How did the best in the world become the best, and learn to battle adversity along the way in reaching their goals? *Daring to Compete* is a handbook for anyone seeking to learn the techniques and thinking behind the world's most successful entrepreneurs.

Jack Cowin, Founder and Executive Chairman,
Competitive Foods Australia

Daring to Compete is a great book for any reader interested in understanding the entrepreneurial mindset around the world. With in-depth and personal interviews of EY Entrepreneur of the Year Country winners, the book identifies the traits of successful entrepreneurs and describes the EY 7 Drivers of Growth™. It's a must read for anyone who aspires to be an entrepreneur!

Judy Chan, CEO, Grace Wine Holdings Ltd., China

How exciting to finally have a book about daring entrepreneurs from different parts of the globe. Their stories, dreams and challenges will be inspiration for future generations of entrepreneurs.

Rebecca MacDonald, Founder and Executive Chair,
Just Energy Group Inc., Canada

Daring to Compete captures the essence of what it takes to be a truly successful entrepreneur in a rapidly evolving global economy. The authors not only break down what it takes to become an entrepreneur, they also share first hand insights from some of today's greatest entrepreneurial success stories.

Michael "Dr. Woody" Woodward, PhD,
Organizational psychologist and author of The YOU Plan
and business media commentator

The world needs more entrepreneurs and people with an entrepreneurial mindset. *Daring to Compete* provides insights into the drivers of growth that successful entrepreneurs must continually develop at every stage of their journey. At Babson, we are educating entrepreneurial leaders who likewise develop an appreciation of what it takes to create great businesses that drive innovation and impact.

Susan G. Duffy, PhD, Executive Director,
The Center for Women's Entrepreneurial Leadership,
Babson College

DARING TO COMPETE

Accelerate Your Business to
Market Leadership with EY's 7 Drivers of Growth™

DARING TO COMPETE

Featuring Insights from Winners of the

EY Entrepreneur
Of The Year™

DIANE FOREMAN | BRYAN PEARCE | GEOFFREY GODDING

EY
Building a better
working world

WILEY

Published by John Wiley & Sons, Inc., Hoboken, New Jersey.
Published simultaneously in Canada.

For general information on our other products and services or for technical support, please contact our Customer Care Department within the United States at (800) 762-2974, outside the United States at (317) 572-3993, or fax (317) 572-4002.

Wiley publishes in a variety of print and electronic formats and by print-on-demand. Some material included with standard print versions of this book may not be included in e-books or in print-on-demand. If this book refers to media such as a CD or DVD that is not included in the version you purchased, you may download this material at http://booksupport.wiley.com. For more information about Wiley products, visit www.wiley.com.

EY Entrepreneur Of The Year, EY World Entrepreneur Of The Year and its associated names and logo's (together the "EOY Name") are proprietary to EY. Any right, title and interest to it belongs to EY.

Library of Congress Cataloging-in-Publication Data

Names: Foreman, Diane, 1960- author. | Pearce , Bryan, 1959- author. |
   Godding, Geoffrey, 1959- author.
Title: Daring to compete : Accelerate Your Business to Market Leadership with EY's 7 Drivers of
   Growth™ / Diane Foreman, Bryan Pearce, Geoffrey Godding.
Description: First Edition. | Hoboken : Wiley, 2019. | Includes index. |
   Identifiers: LCCN 2018046265 (print) | LCCN 2019002637 (ebook) | ISBN
   9781119546818 (ePub) | ISBN 9781119546795 (Adobe PDF) | ISBN 9781119546764
   (hardback) | ISBN 9781119546795 (ePDF)
Subjects: LCSH: Entrepreneurship. | Leadership. | BISAC: BUSINESS & ECONOMICS
   / Entrepreneurship. | BUSINESS & ECONOMICS / General. | BUSINESS &
   ECONOMICS / Leadership.
Classification: LCC HB615 (ebook) | LCC HB615 .F6747 2019 (print) | DDC
   338/.04--dc23
LC record available at https://lccn.loc.gov/2018046265

V10008349_022119

Dedication

Diane Foreman
*For my late husband Bill Foreman, the finest entrepreneur
I ever knew.*

Bryan Pearce
I dedicate my work on Daring to Compete *to my family – my wife
Karen and children Jenny, Scott, and Ali – who have moved around the
world with me, and endured the long hours and many nights away
on business travel for nearly 40 years. Their flexibility has enabled
me to have an exciting career, build relationships with so many
great entrepreneurs, and understand so much about what makes
these entrepreneurs successful and able to drive exceptional
innovation and growth. Thank you!*

*I also want to dedicate this book to the thousands of EY Entrepreneur
Of The Year participants – innovators, creators, and purposeful
leaders who have helped EY to build this important program over
30 years. As coauthors we are the voice to so many colleagues at EY
who have guided, advised, and recognized many of the world's greatest
entrepreneurs. It is the willingness of entrepreneurs and EY colleagues
to share your experiences and insights that make the collective wisdom
contained in the EY 7 Drivers of Growth™ possible.*

Geoffrey Godding

For my family – my wife Madeline and children Henry, Emily, Oliver,
and Annabel – who have endured the consequences of my passion for
what I do. For the incredibly talented and loyal colleagues with whom
I have had the great privilege to work, and for the wonderful clients I
have met and served, many of whom I count as friends, and without
whom I would never have learned anything of real value.

Audere, augere, vincere
[To dare, to strive, to conquer]

Contents

Acknowledgments

Diane Foreman

To EY, thank you for creating and supporting the WEOY program which has allowed tens of thousands of entrepreneurs from every corner of the globe to come together and share their passion and be inspired by each other. You have shown true corporate commitment to "Building a Better Working World."

To Bryan and Geoffrey, thank you for putting your intellectual rigor, good humor, and disciplined debate into this book. Thank you also for spending your working lives supporting entrepreneurs, but most especially thank you for having faith in my intuition. It's been a privilege to work with you.

Bryan Pearce

Daring to Compete would not have been possible without the collaboration of many valued friends and colleagues.

First, we are so grateful to the EY Entrepreneur Of The Year winners from around the world who participated in interviews – opening up and freely sharing their insights and learnings from their amazing entrepreneurial journeys.

Second, to my coauthors Geoffrey Godding – who has provided great leadership around the development and continual refinement of our EY 7 Drivers of Growth™ – and of course to Diane Foreman, an exceptional serial entrepreneur, ardent alumna and supporter of the EY Entrepreneur Of The Year program around the world, and a great friend. Having the perspective of an incredibly successful business builder like Diane has been irreplaceable in developing this book.

To our tireless project manager for this book, Rebekah Craig (Ernst & Young LLP – United States), thanks for all of your dedication and hard work, and to Liz Bolshaw (Ernst & Young – United Kingdom) and Jenni McManus (Ernst & Young – New Zealand) for your editing support.

Geoffrey Godding

Thank you to the teams who helped research, develop, and deploy the EY 7 Drivers of Growth™. The learning from working with them and the many thousands of client interactions that have flowed from these wonderful initiatives have been the fuel for this book.

Thanks also to my coauthors Bryan Pearce, whose knowledge and experience of entrepreneurs is second to none and who epitomizes the spirit of partnership at EY, and to Diane Foreman, who is an unstoppable force of nature, overflowing with insights into the life of an entrepreneur, and is a joy to work with.

Preface

The world needs more entrepreneurs and people with a strong entrepreneurial mind-set, as numerous academic studies have shown.[1] The world needs people who wake up every day, dreaming of building better – better products and services, better companies, better communities, and a better working world.

For more than 30 years, EY has been advising, guiding, and recognizing many of the world's greatest entrepreneurs. Through our work with these entrepreneurs, and hosting the EY Entrepreneur Of The Year program, we have honored and come to understand the stories of thousands of entrepreneurs. At EY, we believe that great businesses of all sizes, including those run by the 15 Entrepreneurs featured in this book, have a strong sense of purpose and are committed to doing their part to build a better working world. Through our commitment to entrepreneurs, and shining the light on their contributions and accomplishments over 30 years, we are proud of our role in helping them to build better.

EY Entrepreneur Of The Year finalists and winners are among the "best of the best" in the world of successful company building. Each year, EY receives nearly 10,000 nominations for great entrepreneurs to be recognized in nearly 145 city

---

[1] Zoltan Acs, "How Is Entrepreneurship Good for Economic Growth?" *Innovations* 1 (2006): 97–107, MIT Press Journals.

or regional programs in more than 50 countries. These nominations are submitted by entrepreneurs, their peers, employees, customers, and suppliers. Nominees don't have to be EY clients: in fact in 2017, less than 20% of nominated companies were our clients. Once nominated, entrepreneurs go through a series of judging rounds – each conducted by independent judges who are typically EY Entrepreneur Of The Year alumni and other entrepreneurs. We believe it takes one to know one, and the selection of award winners by their peers is one of the most meaningful aspects of the program for participants.

For decades, people have asked, "Are entrepreneurs born or made?" Through our interactions with generations of EY Entrepreneur Of The Year contestants and our work with many high-growth entrepreneurs as clients, we have gained exceptional insight into the knowledge and skills it takes to succeed. Through comprehensive research, we have distilled this insight into a framework or toolkit that we call the EY 7 Drivers of Growth™.

We have also seen certain character traits common to the highest-achieving entrepreneurs honored through our program.

In this book we want to share with you both the insights underpinning the EY 7 Drivers of Growth and some exceptional stories that show how builders of market-leading businesses came to create multibillion-dollar companies.

How did the eighth child of a Glasgow butcher, leaving school without qualifications at 16, build a multinational specialist oil and gas equipment manufacturer, now part of one of the largest of its kind in the world?

How did a young New Zealander manage to borrow NZ$1 million to found his company, secured as it was on a leisure park that did not exist, on land he didn't own? And then how did he go on to build that company at an average annual growth rate of 364%?

What was it that propelled a baby girl in Malaysia, abandoned then taken in by a caring stranger, to harness her experience of lying awake listening to the torrential rain beating on the corrugated roof of their shack to build one of the world's premier desalinization companies?

By reading this book, we hope you will be inspired and enlightened to apply entrepreneurial thinking to your business enterprise, wherever you are along your journey toward market leadership.

Diane Foreman, Bryan Pearce, and Geoffrey Godding

Daring to compete – understanding the DNA of entrepreneurs

D ictionary.com defines "dare" as "to have the necessary courage or boldness for something."[1]

Let's face it – being an entrepreneur, founder, and CEO is a lonely job. Your road to market leadership is very difficult to navigate, especially without a reliable road map and the guidance of others who have walked that road and can help you to see around the corners.

Daring to Compete is written to provide entrepreneurs at all stages of their journey – from emerging to market leader – with insights from EY and 15 great business leaders from around the world. These Entrepreneurs (our 15 exemplary EY Entrepreneur Of The Year winners) share their insights on how they develop skills, knowledge, and accelerate their businesses and thrive as entrepreneurial leaders.

The environment in which you operate is changing more rapidly than ever before, and disruption comes at you not only from industry peers but also from new entrants from other sectors that are leveraging innovative technologies and creating new business models. You understand all too well the magnitude of forces that are constantly changing and to which you must respond on a daily basis. These challenges (see Figure P1.1) include:

- Customer preferences and buying behaviors
- Recruiting and retaining top talent
- New competitors, business models, and supply chain implications

---

[1] www.dictionary.com.

3

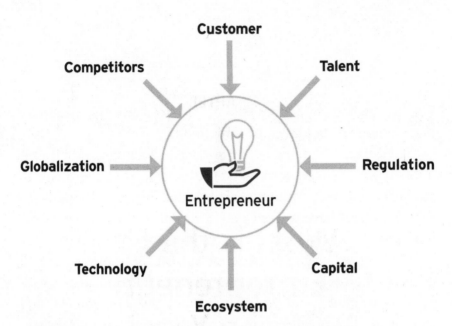

FIGURE P1.1   The environment in which entrepreneurs operate

- Globalization
- Increasing regulation and associated risks of noncompliance
- Disruptive technologies
- Challenges of accessing capital
- Changing ecosystem – mergers, acquisitions, strategic alliances

What sets you apart as an entrepreneur is that every day you are "daring to compete" in the face of these challenges – in fact, you see them as opportunities for accelerating growth. You are unstoppable!

1

What is the EY Entrepreneur Of The Year?

Each year EY receives almost 10,000 nominations from our 145 city or regional programs in over 50 countries, to compete for a range of regional, national, and eventually global titles recognizing exceptional entrepreneurship. Nominations come from multiple sources and less than 20% of them are EY clients. Once nominated, entrepreneurs go through a series of judging rounds – each conducted by independent judges who are typically EY Entrepreneur Of The Year alumni and other entrepreneurs. Ultimately each program annually selects a national winner based on a balanced scorecard of key criteria that together reflect the essence of a truly great entrepreneur. These are, in no particular order:

- Entrepreneurial spirit
- Value creation
- Strategic direction
- National and global impact
- Innovation
- Personal integrity / purpose-driven leadership

Each June, national winners representing more than 50 nations come to Monaco to represent their country at the world's premier event that recognizes and celebrates entrepreneurial achievement. While there, they participate in a final round of independent judging. Ultimately, one is named the EY World Entrepreneur Of The Year™ – a highly coveted honor. The prize isn't monetary: it is the recognition of exceptional achievement by a group of respected peers. Together the entrepreneurs participating in the EY World

Entrepreneur Of The Year 2018 competition in Monaco had the characteristics shown in Figure 1.1.

Over the history of the competition, winners have included individuals such as Guy Laliberté of Cirque du Soleil in Canada, Wayne Huizenga (who created multiple companies including Blockbuster Video and Waste Management, Inc.) in the United States, Mohed Altrad of the Altrad Group in France, and Olivia Lum of Hyflux in Singapore. We hope you are inspired to join them by applying to your local EY Entrepreneur Of The Year program (details are contained in the Appendix).

Combined revenues of approximately US$23b

Average revenues of US$500m

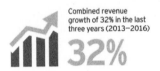
Combined revenue growth of 32% in the last three years (2013–2016) 32%

Award
Rubens Menin
MRV Engenharia, Brazil
EY World Entrepreneur Of The Year 2018

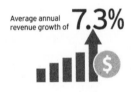
Average annual revenue growth of 7.3%

110,217 employees combined with job growth of **9.2%** between 2013 and 2016

FIGURE 1.1 Key statistics on the entrepreneurs who competed at the EY World Entrepreneur of the Year 2018

What are the EY 7 Drivers of Growth™?

"**E**Y's 7 Drivers of Growth is a powerful management framework that enables business leaders to benchmark themselves against global, cross-industry leading practices," says Ryan Burke, EY Global Leader, Growth Markets. "Importantly, it also helps them build their growth plan to deliver against their strategic objectives."

Through our interactions with these great EY Entrepreneur Of The Year contestants, observing the selection process carried out by our judges (all of whom are independent of EY), and our work with many high-growth entrepreneurs as clients, we have obtained deep insight into the knowledge and skills these women and men use to drive sustainable growth. Through comprehensive research, we have distilled this insight into what we refer to as the EY 7 Drivers of Growth™ (see Figure 2.1).

First and foremost, successful entrepreneurs who achieve sustainable high growth have an unrelenting focus on the Customer. They put customers at the center of everything they do. To achieve optimal customer satisfaction, these entrepreneurs also invest time and capital on six additional areas: People, behaviors, and culture; Digital technology and analytics; Operations; Funding and finance; Transactions and alliances; and Risk.

These world-class entrepreneurs also understand the importance of *maintaining balance* between these drivers as they grow sustainable companies. For example, a leader who focuses only on current sales to customers without building a great team and culture and putting in place adequate funding and finance to support the growth will quickly find his or her company unable to deliver on its promises.

Journey to Market Leadership

Accelerated Growth

People, behaviors, and culture
Digital technology and analytics
Operations
Customer
Funding and finance
Transactions and alliances
Risk

FIGURE 2.1 The EY 7 Drivers of Growth

Our research also shows that as successful entrepreneurial companies move toward market leadership, they generally progress through three stages: Developing, Established, and ultimately Leading. They may move through these stages with varying speed, but will follow a similar pathway. While the specific activities that successful entrepreneurial businesses must focus on within each of the 7 Drivers of Growth will vary somewhat in each of these stages, many are common across the board.

This research that led to the EY 7 Drivers of Growth validated our firsthand understanding, obtained through thousands of interactions and face-to-face sessions with entrepreneurs and business leaders around the world.

These entrepreneurs have spent their lives continually daring to compete. For them, there is no finish line – their days are spent looking for ways to compete more effectively, innovate, diversify, and seize on the exciting opportunities that present themselves as a result of industry convergence and new technologies. Through our interviews, in addition to sharing their inspiring, transformational stories, they have explained ways that they have adopted these 7 Drivers of Growth in guiding their companies to success. As the EY Entrepreneur Of The Year® 2016 winner for the United States, J.W. Marriott Jr. notes, "Success is never final."

We hope that the EY 7 Drivers of Growth model becomes an indispensable road map you will use on your journey to market leadership.

3

Do you have the E-gene?

What is an entrepreneur? The dictionary definition is "a person who organizes and manages any enterprise, especially a business, usually with considerable initiative and risk."[1]

But that's far from the whole story!

Entrepreneurs don't just run businesses – they create, expand, and redesign them. They risk the unproven to realize and constantly evolve the future.

Entrepreneurs don't just make and supply products and services – they imagine them and constantly adapt them to meet existing and anticipated customer needs.

Entrepreneurs don't just meet the demands of markets and existing customers – they adapt markets and they create new customers. They expand, diversify, and evolve.

Entrepreneurs don't sleep – they dream. And they take risks to see their dreams become reality.

An entrepreneur's business is never a "done deal" – like entrepreneurs themselves, it's always a work in progress.

For decades, people have asked, "Are entrepreneurs made or born?" Unquestionably, they are born with a "spark." Successful entrepreneurs fan that spark and continually strengthen their entrepreneurial "muscle."

Through the EY World Entrepreneur Of The Year program, we have the privilege of getting to know many of the world's finest entrepreneurs.

"Those who have been independently selected as EY Entrepreneur Of The Year winners and finalists from their peers over the more than 30 years our program has been in existence are

---

[1] www.dictionary.com.

truly exemplary," says Ryan Burke, EY Global Leader, Growth Markets. "These CEOs, owners, and founders typify not only business-building at its best, but they do so with a clear sense of purpose and commitment to building a better working world. I have met many of these winners personally and see firsthand their qualities as world-class leaders. In addition – many have become my own mentors and friends."

To showcase entrepreneurship at its best, we have selected a cross section of 15 entrepreneurial superstars who do everything from fast food delivery to curing cancer. We selected them because they have been recognized by their peers for their outstanding achievements. Six of the 15 were named EY World Entrepreneur Of The Year: the very pinnacle of the competition. We also selected them to portray a diverse group in every sense – gender, ethnicity, religious beliefs, industry sector, and geography. This is by design – great entrepreneurs come in all shapes and sizes.

The Entrepreneurs we interviewed are:

- Rubens Menin, MRV Engenharia, Brazil, EY World Entrepreneur Of The Year 2018
- Murad Al-Katib, AGT Food and Ingredients, Canada, EY World Entrepreneur Of The Year 2017
- Manny Stul, Moose Toys, Australia, EY World Entrepreneur Of The Year 2016
- Mohed Altrad, The Altrad Group, France, EY World Entrepreneur Of The Year 2015
- Ilkka Paananen, Supercell, EY Entrepreneur Of The Year 2015 Finland
- Rosario Bazán, DanPer, EY Entrepreneur Of The Year 2014 Peru
- Linda Hasenfratz, Linamar Corporation, EY Entrepreneur Of The Year 2014 Canada

- Craig Heatley, Founder, Rainbow Corporation and SKY TV, EY Entrepreneur Of The Year 2012 New Zealand
- Dr. Mary Lynne Hedley and Lonnie Moulder, TESARO, Inc., EY Entrepreneur Of The Year® 2017 United States
- Uday Kotak, Kotak Mahindra Bank, India, EY World Entrepreneur Of The Year 2014
- Michael Wu, Maxim Group, EY Entrepreneur Of The Year 2012 Hong Kong
- Olivia Lum, Hyflux Ltd., Singapore, EY World Entrepreneur Of The Year 2011
- Jim Nixon, Nixon Energy Investments, EY Entrepreneur Of The Year 2010 United States – Manufacturing and Distribution winner Southwest Region, and EY World Entrepreneur Of The Year Judge (2016–2018, the latter two years as Chair)
- Dame Rosemary Squire, Trafalgar Entertainment Group Ltd. and co-founder of Ambassador Theatre Group ("ATG"), EY Entrepreneur Of The Year 2014 United Kingdom

In the course of the past year we traveled the world, spending time with each of these remarkable winners. We asked questions and most importantly, we listened.

What did we learn?

- Entrepreneurs see the world differently from how others see it. They dream about and look for opportunities.
- Entrepreneurs have an urge to live life to the full – with passion, focus, confidence, hard work, courage, guts, and the ability to learn from failure. They are unstoppable.

For the Entrepreneurs that we interviewed for this book, it isn't about making money – in fact, their primary motivation is the thrill and challenge of growing an idea into a thriving business. They might make a lot of money, but that's not in itself the end-game; it's just the scorecard by which others may judge them. The real endgame is that money buys the freedom to control their own lives and allows them to fulfill their passion for soci-etal impact. Every entrepreneur we met is committed to creating a better working world and improving the lives and communi-ties of people in need.

We noted many similarities in the traits and characteristics of the Entrepreneurs, something that is in their collective DNA. Per-haps it is the "entrepreneurial gene" – the "E-gene" – that gives them their competitive advantage. As Uday Kotak says, "I think entrepreneurship is in my DNA and my natural entrepreneurial instinct is deep within me." Olivia Lum puts it another way: "I feel that you can't develop into an entrepreneur. I know that even at a young age I would develop an idea, sleep on it, and dream about it. Somehow, it's already part of your DNA. As an entrepreneur your eyes are always open. Every day as a small child I had my antenna up looking for free food and being an entrepreneur is the same…I don't think you can develop entrepreneurship – it must be in you. You always have to ask yourself whether you are an entrepreneur, or simply a good manager? I sometimes look at younger entrepreneurs and they have good ideas, but is a good idea enough to make someone passionate?"

This book is a compilation of the collective wisdom of some of the best entrepreneurs in the world. Natural-born entre-preneurs reading this will be further inspired and will learn to strengthen their entrepreneurial muscle. As golf legend Jack Nicklaus is quoted as saying, "Confidence is the most impor-tant single factor in this game, and no matter how great your natural talent, there is only one way to obtain and sustain it: work." Professional managers, who perhaps are not natural-born entrepreneurs and who, like the Tin Man in *The Wizard of Oz*, are missing the heart (of an entrepreneur), can read this book to learn how to develop a strong entrepreneurial mind-set.

This entrepreneurial mind-set comprises key traits or attributes that we see in all our high-achieving Entrepreneurs. While some of these traits can be found in the best corporate leaders, rarely do professional managers possess them to the extent commonly found in entrepreneurs.

Passion

"To succeed you must have dedicated commitment, discipline, and above all passion," says Alfred Pisani, founder and chairman of the Corinthia Group and Entrepreneur Of The Year 2017 Malta.

Passion is written into the code of the entrepreneurs' DNA; it empowers them to found new enterprises and drives them along the journey to market leadership. As Jim Nixon says, "Follow your passion and never ever give up, never let go."

Even when successful entrepreneurs sell their businesses, their passion doesn't get sold. They simply take it to another aspect of their lives or go right back to starting all over again. Craig Heatley, Entrepreneur of the Year 2012 New Zealand, "retired" for the first time at 29. He had just sold Rainbow Corporation and never needed to work again. He says of retirement, "It sounds great to be able to go and play golf every day but your friends can't do that – they were out working.... So I got bored and within weeks I realized this wasn't fun anymore." Heatley directed his energy and resources to create SKY TV, one of the largest companies ever listed on the New Zealand stock exchange. And after retiring from SKY TV, he took his passion for golf and put it to work. He now sits on the board of the Master's Golf Tournament and chairs its media committee.

Murad Al-Katib, World Entrepreneur Of The Year 2017, explains, "Passion, passion, passion – to me it's not only about liking what you do – that undersells. When I meet great entrepreneurs in the world, whether they are small or large, you detect a passion for what they do, their causes, their businesses, and their products."

Some of the other Entrepreneurs see passion as an element that motivates and sustains them – it's what gets them out of bed in the morning and keeps them going through times of inevitable challenge.

Manny Stul, World Entrepreneur Of The Year 2016, says, "I think it's important for everyone to find a passion that they love to get up in the morning and do. It doesn't matter what it is. I just happen to really enjoy business, in particular this business."

Olivia Lum, World Entrepreneur Of The Year 2011, says, "Entrepreneurship must also come with patience, persistence, and probably passion. Despite big challenges you still have to be passionate."

Without passion, you will never have the drive to fuel belief in yourself and your enterprise, and to infect all who work with you with the same enthusiasm.

Drive

"There is no question, I am driven. It could have been my background. It could be the poor environment I was brought up in. It could have been a whole variety of things, but I am very driven and I am very competitive," says Manny Stul, Moose Toys, and World Entrepreneur Of The Year 2016. "I played a lot of sport when I was younger and just desperately wanted to win – it was very important to me. It wasn't so much other people's perception of me, it was how I felt about myself. It's the same in business – it's just being driven to succeed."

It's almost a cliché that entrepreneurs are highly driven and motivated individuals. They are driven in everything they do in life. Typically highly competitive, they seek to win every battle. They strive to be better, bigger, and faster than the competition. This drive is fueled by a burning ambition to create value and better themselves. This ambition is rarely satisfied. When they achieve their immediate goals, they reset those goals, recalibrate, and start again, always pushing the boundaries of what is possible for them and all those around them. This drive is never diminished by failure – indeed it is further enhanced by a determination to learn from mistakes, do it again, and succeed. It is highly infectious and contributes significantly to the attraction, development, and retention of top talent. Unquestionably, it is a major contributor to top performance at every level in their business.

Agility

Great entrepreneurs are known for their agility in decision making and execution.

Entrepreneurs are wired to be agile. They don't want to be caught up in long decision-making processes; they want to say "go" and see something happen.

Agility is the ability to respond quickly to change. As Ilkka Paananen, Supercell and Entrepreneur Of The Year 2015 Finland, says, "Get big by thinking small. We value the speed of small teams and keeping things simple."

Even when the company becomes large, entrepreneurial thinking is behind its growth.

"Perhaps the best piece of advice I received as an entrepreneur is, "Think big, act small, move quickly and smartly," agrees Linda Hasenfratz, Linamar Corporation and Entrepreneur Of The Year 2014 Canada.

Inspirational leadership

Entrepreneurs are by their nature leaders. They have little choice. They are convinced that there is a better way of solving a problem, filling a niche, meeting a need, and this drives them to the front, not following from the back. And to realize their dreams, exceptional entrepreneurs tend to be charismatic leaders: able to infect others with their enthusiasm and conviction. As Martin Luther King Jr. famously said, "A genuine leader is not a searcher for consensus, but a molder of consensus."

Team building and motivating

Entrepreneurs are inspirational leaders and often only adequate managers or administrators. An inspiring leader creates high performing teams and motivates those teams to accomplish great things.

As Manny Stul puts it, "It has to come from the top. You can't just put up 10 points and say, 'this is what we are going to do' and then not actually believe and live it – because the people working with you get what's going on and you can't fool them. You might be able to fool them in the short term, but you are not going to fool them long term. So you must actually live what you believe."

An inspirational leader provides a high-growth environment, infuses the organization with passion, and communicates a plan that ensures the best and brightest want to be part of the dream. "A team that is dedicated, ethical, and passionate about what they do are genuine dream makers," says Rubens Menin, World Entrepreneur Of The Year 2018.

The Entrepreneurs all agree that it's the team that matters more than any individual. They want to hire and learn from people who are better than they are. Great entrepreneurs add people to their teams who bring knowledge and experience as well as relevant networks.

"When you are a young entrepreneur you can do a lot yourself but there comes a point in your business where you must decide that you can no longer have the sphere of influence," says Jim Nixon. "To continue the growth, you must bring people into the business who are smarter than you and win them over to believe in the vision. With every new person, you are expanding your sphere of influence and the sphere of influence for your vision of the direction of the company. I think my biggest attribute was that I was able to bring a team of highly talented, high-quality people with me."

Great entrepreneurs themselves make a big impact, and they know how to bring high-impact players onto their teams – people who get results and thrive in the culture the entrepreneur has set.

Ilkka Paananen, Entrepreneur of the Year 2015 Finland, puts it this way, "The best environment is one where these people and teams can make the biggest possible impact. There is no friction that would slow down or would prevent them from being successful."

When Craig Heatley is building a team, he looks for "flexibility, honesty, integrity and enthusiasm."

Relationship building

In addition to building great teams, the Entrepreneurs actively build great relationships in their ecosystem of peers, investors, customers, and partners. They not only build their own relationships, but also encourage their teams to build strategic relationships with their peers and others in the broader ecosystem.

Linda Hasenfratz believes in "the importance of relation-ship building at all levels of the organization within my own team and between my team, customers, and other stakeholders."

Diversity of relationships across the leadership of the organization will help to truly understand the needs of all stakeholders.

Mary Lynne Hedley and Lonnie Moulder say, "One of the challenges can be that we are all motivated differently, and we have to understand people and identify what their barriers to success are.... It's probably true of any business to under-stand what each party needs for success and then to enable each party to be successful. And that sometimes means you have to compromise."

Humility and confidence

Another very important, although perhaps surprising, trait of the Entrepreneurs is that they are humble due in part to a degree of self-doubt.

"One thing that keeps me awake at night is a simple question, 'Will I have a bank the next morning?'" says Uday Kotak. He never takes success as a given. "Just because you have succeeded in the past, don't think that success is to be taken for granted, and therefore always have the humility to accept the fact that even if you are making a judgment call, you can go wrong. So if you have that humility and if you are factoring that into your overall scheme of things, you can move forward."

Entrepreneurs are driven by a need for continual improve-ment and appear to have a high degree of self-confidence – but in reality this is offset by a degree of self-doubt that leads to continual questioning and a quest to make things better. Keep-ing confidence and self-doubt in equilibrium is one of the many character traits that mark out entrepreneurs.

Vision and focus

"Entrepreneurship is a way of life that requires persistence, innovation, and the ability to influence people with your vision," says Ziv Aviram, co-founder of MobilEye and Entrepreneur Of The Year 2016 Israel.

The Entrepreneurs all exhibit great vision – the ability to dream to see trends and the big picture, to be innovators and risk-takers. They also have the ability to focus and chart a clear course for execution to exploit the opportunity.

Being an entrepreneur and having simultaneous vision and focus is like being the conductor of an orchestra. The conductor interprets the music and shares the vision to inspire the musicians to deliver. The conductor is constantly thinking ahead in the score, while simultaneously listening and watching all the parts of the orchestra performing.

"Look ahead and see yourself there already, never be afraid to follow your own beliefs and make a dream a reality," says Sami Sagol, Keter Group and Entrepreneur Of The Year 2017 Israel. "By having a strong personal vision, you can achieve goals that no one has ever anticipated."

This thinking is hard-wired into all market-leading entrepreneurs.

Entrepreneurs are dreamers but see the risks too – they don't just look for a gap in a market; they also ensure there is a market in the gap.

While an innovative and clearly articulated vision is a hallmark of successful entrepreneurs, it is also essential to be able to focus on execution – turning the vision into reality. As Thomas Edison said, success is "1% inspiration and 99% perspiration."

Focus involves choosing from the many opportunities that constantly present and being able to say "yes" to some, and maximize value from them, while also saying "no" to others, in order to devote scarce resources to projects that will have the greatest impact and yield. Ilkka Paananen says, "In my mind, quality and focus go hand-in-hand, and the hardest thing about focus is not to say what you do but to say what you do not do – i.e., saying 'no' to interesting ideas. I believe the only way to achieve the highest possible quality is to be very focused, which means saying 'no' a lot."

Intense focus also enables entrepreneurs and their teams to identify opportunities for innovation that others may miss. Mohed Altrad, World Entrepreneur Of The Year 2015 says, "The biggest lesson is being focused because that is where the benefit lies. I can see people's reactions. You learn a lot about human nature and human reaction where other people can't find a solution."

A hunger for learning

"In today's fast-changing environment, nobody knows nothing," says Ambarish Mitra, founder of Blippar and Entrepreneur Of The Year 2017 United Kingdom. "It's your own firsthand experience that teaches you the most."

While some of the Entrepreneurs have attended the best schools and obtained post-doctorates, doctorates, master's degrees, and MBAs, others are "QBE" – "qualified by experience." Education is not what defines them. These Entrepreneurs agree that being interested and interesting is much more important than where you went to school and what degrees you obtained.

The Entrepreneurs exhibit a natural curiosity and an insatiable hunger for continuous learning. They want to understand what works, what doesn't, and why. They learn from all sources at all levels of the business, frequently seen at the coalface talking with the people in their business who, in their eyes, really know what's happening internally, and with customers, suppliers, and other stakeholders.

Michael Wu's perspective is typical: "As a leader it is important to stay grounded and know what is going on in the front line. I spend on average two days a week visiting stores. I talk to the manager, kitchen staff, crew, and even the customers. Understanding and filtering what they tell me and how they feel shapes some of the most important decisions I make for the company."

Successful entrepreneurs learn from each other and from their teams – they don't need to be the smartest or best-educated people in the room or at the board table. "I think it's absolutely essential to have people who are smarter than you," says Jim Nixon. Everybody says that but not so many people do it. My view is that I only bet on smart people."

"Smart" does not necessarily correspond to formal training. Successful entrepreneurs look for "smart" in a variety of ways: previous experience – increasingly to harness cross-sector innovation, creative problem solving, diversity and skills, and knowledge, which complement and augment what already exists within the current team. Craig Heatley agrees, "I have always been cognizant of what I don't know, which is lots. It was Thomas Edison who said 'we don't know one millionth of 1% of anything.' I have always believed that, so I've been more than happy to go out and find people with the knowledge that can help, whatever the destination."

Entrepreneurs are inherently interested in others. They are always asking the where, what, and why questions. They talk very little about themselves but dig deep when talking to others.

Learning from failure

The great adage attributed to author and speaker John C. Maxwell could have been designed for entrepreneurs: "sometimes you win; sometimes you learn."

All entrepreneurs have suffered some crushing defeats but they all have the ability to quickly recover from failure as an essential part of their DNA. Entrepreneurs often remark that they learn more from their failures than from their successes, and simply see failure as a necessary component on the path to success. As Ilkka Paananen says, "I want to invest in people who are not afraid to take risks and fail, but rather see failure as an inevitable and necessary path toward creating successful products and services. If you just play it safe, you will never achieve anything big."

Dame Rosemary Squire says, "You don't learn anything until you get it wrong and then you think: I am not going to do that again."

Entrepreneurs learn from failure but then move on. "If you have a problem, deal with it," says Mohed Altrad. "Go through all the facts and whatever you can find out about how to resolve it, but once you have made a decision and explored all the options, stop worrying about it."

Resilience

"Success is when you recover from failure and perform at a whole new level," says Jozsef Varadi, Wizz Air and Entrepreneur Of The Year 2017 Hungary.

Resilience is defined as the "ability to recover readily from…adversity or the like."[2] The Entrepreneurs have all faced adversity of some form in both their personal and business lives, yet they display various traits or attributes that illustrate their resilience.

---

[2] www.dictionary.com.

Dame Rosemary Squire, the first woman to win the EY Entrepreneur Of The Year award for the United Kingdom, says, "Personal adversity and challenges of all kinds – and let's face it most people have them – do drive you. They create resilience, you must survive, and you have to find a way. For an entrepreneur, resilience is an extremely important quality. I think the things that have gone wrong in my life have made me more resilient and more able to be imaginative, so that when situations arise I am now able to see solutions."

Values focused

Values – our ideals, raison d'être, and moral compass – are formed by our family upbringing, our education, and our life experiences. The Entrepreneurs have clearly defined values and these shape their company purpose and culture and provide them with a "true north" in the midst of a difficult situation.

Rosario Bazán, Entrepreneur Of The Year 2014 Peru, says, "The lesson I drew was that even in the darkest of times, if you stay true to yourself and your values, you will overcome any situation."

Sometimes values combine to support resilience in adversity, particularly if those values derive from religious belief. "I am a believer," says Olivia Lum. "I am a Christian, so being a believer has helped me a lot. My constant companion is my Bible and that has also encouraged me. I am not alone. I have the heavenly Father who loves me more than anyone else does."

No one explains values better than Mohed Altrad when he says, "We are brothers, we are sisters, and we must all love each other every day. Believe in yourself, believe in the future."

Societal impact

Entrepreneurs also have a strong sense of obligation to make a positive societal impact and embed that into their culture and business model.

"I believe we'll have a better working world when a company mission can inspire an ordinary group of people to do extraordinary things, when a set of corporate values exemplifies how those people engage with each other and their customers, when ideas are more important than position or credentials, and the purpose of the work people do becomes more important than any one individual," says Mary Lynne Hedley of TESARO Inc. and Entrepreneur Of The Year 2017 United States. This paragraph could serve as a mantra for our vision of entrepreneurship and the reason that we are so committed to being alongside of entrepreneurs who are committed to building a better world.

"I think purpose is extremely crucial," says Uday Kotak, Kotak Mahindra Bank and EY World Entrepreneur Of The Year 2014. "I can say that since starting my company in 1985, I have enjoyed every single day of the past 33 years and there is a sense of mission, of building and creating something which is what drives me every single day, so it's got nothing to do with work time – there is no difference between work and nonwork because my mind is deeply involved in going out there and building something, which effectively lasts beyond us.

"My drive for purpose started when I made my first trip to the United States and I saw these phenomenal institutions called J.P. Morgan, Morgan Stanley, Merrill Lynch, Goldman Sachs, and here I was with this very little company which started in India with three people. So, I asked myself, 'why can't we build an institution maybe started by an individual or a family which could outlast those individuals?'"

Having the "E-Gene" means that entrepreneurs care not just about themselves and their businesses but about society and the world. They are driven by purpose and committed to giving back. Manny Stul has "strong convictions about community responsibility" and sees it as a privilege to donate across a wide variety of philanthropic efforts, giving 10% of his income to not-for-profit organizations in Australia and worldwide.

Likewise Ilkka Paananen and his team place a lot of importance on sharing the benefits of their financial success. They have donated millions of dollars to charitable causes, ranging from a children's hospital in Helsinki to fighting AIDS across Africa.

For many, it goes beyond financial support alone, by leveraging the networks and capabilities of their businesses to make a direct impact, as evidenced, for example, by Murad Al-Katib, who has donated millions of food ration packages to refugees, which include his own food products.

Our outstanding Entrepreneurs care that their entire value chain is ethical and fair, but more than this, they strive to ensure that they leave everything they touch in a better state than they found it.

These traits of successful entrepreneurs are summarized in Figure 3.1.

These entrepreneurs are amazing people! They are inspirational leaders, visionary, hungry to learn, resilient, values-focused, and agile. These traits equip them to succeed as they are daring to compete. We discovered that their entrepreneurial DNA also contains another unique ingredient. As you read through this book – the stories and the insights from the Entrepreneurs – can you spot it? Ask yourself – what is it and do you have the "E-gene"?

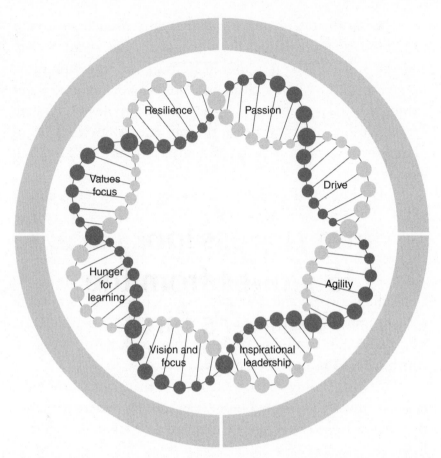

FIGURE 3.1 Summary: "Traits of successful entrepreneurs"

What success looks like: 15 stories from the "Winner's Circle"

In Part 2 we include biographical sketches of the 15 award-winning Entrepreneurs that we interviewed in depth for this book.[1] They are grouped by geography: the Americas, Asia Pacific, the United Kingdom, and Europe. We selected these 15 partly to show that extraordinary entrepreneurs are born in any country, from any background, operating in any sector. Their stories are stories of individuals but they also provide us with archetypes from which every aspiring entrepreneur can learn. As sectors converge with the disruptive force of new cognitive technologies, it is easier than ever to apply insights from success in one sector to another.

In each case we show how these exceptional people have used an understanding of the EY 7 Drivers of Growth, sometimes intuitively, to build their businesses from the developing stage to market leading. In Chapters 4–6, the driver which is being illustrated has been bolded.

Part 3 includes more detailed chapters on each of the 7 Drivers of Growth and how they interact with and support each other.

Finally, in Part 4, we show how the entrepreneurial traits we describe in Part 1 – the E-gene – translate into specific entrepreneurial behaviors as illustrated by our Entrepreneurs.

While you may feel humbled by these stories, we hope you will be inspired to take your business to the next level.

---

[1] Excerpts from selected video interviews with the Entrepreneurs can be seen at www.ey.com/daringtocompete.

Entrepreneurs based in the Americas

MURAD AL-KATIB
AGT FOOD AND
INGREDIENTS INC.
EY WORLD
ENTREPRENEUR OF
THE YEAR 2017
CANADA

I magine a world without hunger – a world where everyone can eat safe, affordable, and sustainable protein.

That's the aim of Murad Al-Katib, whose AGT Food and Ingredients Inc. (AGT) – the world's largest vertically integrated supply chain for lentils, chickpeas, and peas ("pulses") – is playing its part in growing the world's plant-based protein supply. "In the next 40 years," says Murad, "we have to produce as much food as we produced in the past 10,000 years of civilization. That is a great challenge for the world. But in this challenge there is also opportunity."

Murad was born a first-generation Canadian in rural Saskatchewan, Canada. Even as a five-year-old starting school, Murad's entrepreneurial spirit was strong. He was more excited by the fact he now had a "store" to sell the bubble gum (sourced from his family's native Turkey during trips back home to visit relatives) than he was about his education. He also had a gut feeling that there was a big world outside his small town and he had a burning desire to "figure out how to be part of that world."

Sometime around the age of 12 or 13, Murad realized he would not be following the previous five generations of Al-Katib family men, all of whom had become doctors. Medical school and taking over his father's practice was "almost a foregone conclusion" but Murad was interested in business and had the gift of gab. "I think the transition from aspiring doctor to entrepreneur really started at that point." At the same time, he was developing his leadership and mentoring skills. Realizing, at around 16, that he was a better sports coach than a player, he began coaching community hockey and baseball. These coaching skills would hold him in good stead when it came to putting his business plan into action.

Following the example of his parents, who quickly became leaders in their town of 1,200 people, Murad developed a passion for economic development and agriculture. "The opportunity was there to take our farming communities, transform the crops they grew, and match them to what the world demanded," he says. That demand is for protein – enough to feed 10 billion people by 2025. "It drove me to do something that would create that wealth in the communities in which I lived," he says, "and also to be part of feeding the world." The vision was simple: to build a global processing company to export pulses grown on Canada's rural prairies. The business would become the strategic link between producers and the rest of the world.

The epiphany was his realization that in a food-starved, water-starved world, producing plant protein was infinitely more sustainable than farming animals. It takes only 43 gallons of water to produce a pound of lentils, compared with 1,850 gallons to produce a pound of beef. Murad saw this as his opportunity to not only create a global, sustainable, and highly profitable food business but also as a way to " give back" on a scale that even he was finding difficult to envisage.

It was not necessarily an ideal time to start a business. Murad had a government job that paid well and his wife, Michelle, was pregnant with twins. Nonetheless, Murad and Michelle mortgaged their home, emptied their savings account, and begged and borrowed from family and friends. AGT was born two months before their twins. "I told my wife that if the business succeeded to a point where it was viable, we would continue," he says. "If not, I could always go and work for someone else again."

Early on, Murad realized that while he had a great idea, a good education, and passion, he also needed **transactions and alliances** with strategic partners who could bring operations experience and provide funding. He identified Arbel, a Turkish company owned by the Arslan family, as a possible partner. They were experienced lentil processors and were prepared to invest US$1 million in his embryonic company. Not only did the business become viable, but six years later Murad bought the Arslan's family business for US$104 million. Murad credits his family values – part of the commitment to **people, behaviors, and culture** that he wove into the fabric of AGT – "for ensuring the Arslans have become part of my family as well as remaining partners." In fact, he says, what has made him so passionate about his business and "who I am" comes down to family values. "I credit my mum, dad, and wife for that. My management team is not only my management team; they are my best friends."

Today, AGT is a multinational company with annual revenue of US$1.49 billion, operating 47 facilities around the globe.

It has 2,000 employees, serving customers in 120 countries on five continents, and exports about 23% of the world trade in lentils. In 2009 it listed on the Canadian Stock Exchange.

Sir Winston Churchill rightly said, "The price of greatness is responsibility." Murad has embraced this philosophy. In 2017, Murad was named EY World Entrepreneur Of The Year – a remarkable achievement in itself – and his philanthropic work was also recognized by a committee of Nobel Laureates in Peace and Economic Science, who awarded him the coveted Oslo Business for Peace award.

The previous year Murad was named Global Citizen Laureate by the United Nations Association of Canada after using his global supply chain, manufacturing, and distribution systems to produce and deliver more than four million family ration cartons for Syrian refugees, some of the world's most vulnerable people. In 2017, Murad was honored with the Saskatchewan Order of Merit, joining an elite annual group recognized for excellence, achievement, and contributions to the well-being of the province of Saskatchewan and its residents. PROFIT Guide magazine named him one of Canada's best entrepreneurs of the past 30 years, and Queen Elizabeth II awarded him a Diamond Jubilee medal for his work as an entrepreneur and job creator.

*   *   *

While these awards are a "nice to have, " Murad says what drives him is not a desire for international fame and recognition but the knowledge that the world must grow more food. He struggled at first with the idea of making a profit from supplying food to vulnerable people but realized that he had a business to run, a responsibility to shareholders, and the need to generate a return. This return ultimately sustains the ability of the company to do good.

ROSARIO BAZÁN
DANPER
EY ENTREPRENEUR OF
THE YEAR 2014
PERU

A leading female entrepreneur from Latin America, Rosario Bazán, cofounder and CEO of DanPer, is building one of Latin America's leading agribusinesses. DanPer is one of Peru's biggest producers and exporters of nontraditional agricultural products, such as asparagus, artichokes, peppers, grapes, avocados, mangoes, and blueberries. It also produces super-grains such as quinoa – both as a grain and in ready-to-eat meals – which are exported to supermarkets around the world. As she builds DanPer, she is also building on the skills and economic prospects of thousands of her fellow Peruvians.

Rosario Bazán, the cofounder and CEO of Peruvian agribusiness DanPer, credits many of her entrepreneurial skills to the lessons she learned growing up as the eighth child in a family of 11 children (all of whom obtained university degrees), and her parents, who put great store on ethics and values such as reliability, integrity, honesty, care, and responsibility for disadvantaged members of their community.

Rosario got her fighting spirit from her mother, who is 92 years old, and from her father, who is 96, she learned to respect people for who they are – not for what they have.

The values and skills she acquired as a child stood her in good stead when, several years later, Rosario and husband Jorge Aranguri faced the collapse of their first business, a pineapple exporting venture, as the Peruvian economy hit the wall in the late 1980s.

It was the most challenging time of her life, Rosario says, but something great came from the experience. Although hyperinflation had forced her to close the business, Rosario continued to honor her commitments to employees, suppliers, and customers.

Rosario shares with a great level of faith that the love of God has always been with her and that she feels that her best strategic partner has been Jesus. Over time, her faith and strong trust in God has been her greatest source of spiritual and emotional strength to face adversities and challenges.

Rather than emigrating, like so many of her compatriots in the wake of the Peruvian financial crisis, the pair decided to remain in their homeland and fight for a better country. So impressed were their Danish partners that Rosario and Jorge were offered the opportunity of starting a new venture, and in 1994 they formed DanPer, reflecting the names of the two nations, and based in the northern Peruvian city of Trujillo.

Transactions and alliances have been one of the factors of DanPer's success – notably their strategic partnership, which is even stronger 24 years later. "It was not a matter of luck," she says, "but more a matter of being really aware of whomever we were making our partnership with. The relationship has become more solid and we are very much prepared to face the new challenges that will come with the next generation."

In addition to establishing a strong strategic partnership, Rosario determined to focus on **people, behaviors, and culture** – the people who would make her company one of Peru's business success stories, promoting the development of their capabilities, providing them with access to free health services inside the processing plants and on the agricultural fields, and supplying permanent training and educational opportunities. DanPer also promotes a culture of career-long learning – including sending managers abroad for formal training and encouraging them to study for MBAs. Rosario also implemented internal gender equality practices, while ensuring all promotions are based strictly on merit. More than 60% of DanPer's employees are women, many of whom are the principal family breadwinners. As Rosario puts it, "When a woman takes a step forward, society as a whole advances."

Rosario has also focused on expanding the geographic **customer** base of DanPer, now exporting to more than 30 countries on five continents and diversifying its product family. DanPer is among the three largest agricultural exporters in Peru. It is the world's largest exporter of artichokes and operates across Peru's three distinct geographical zones – the Coast, the Andes, and the Amazon – no mean feat in a nation with challenging topography and a significant deficit in transport infrastructure.

As a woman CEO working in provincial Peru, Rosario is used to breaking the mold. She has a passion for innovation, saying the innovation of products, processes, and business models is a key element in DanPer's growth and development. "**Operating** in a fiercely competitive business environment, we are challenged to develop competitive advantages based on innovation to improve our productivity and profitability," she says.

But profitability is not the main driver for Rosario. Since DanPer's inception, she has built a long-term vision of environmental and social sustainability, as well as holding the conviction that building an ethical, successful, and world-renowned company is the most effective way of contributing to Peru's national development and the alleviation of poverty.

Rosario and Jorge launched DanPer with 150 staff and sales in their first year of US$3.5 million. It now employs more than 10,000 people while indirectly providing work for another 15,000 people, almost all living in impoverished rural areas where previously there has been little or no formal employment.

DanPer's strict ethics, exemplary sustainability policies, and strong commitment to its workers and host communities have made it a national role model of corporate responsibility. The company leads literacy and public health campaigns, including providing free health care to neighboring communities.

Rosario is a former president of the Cámara de Comercio de La Libertad and president of the Asociación de Agricultores Agroexportadores Propietarios de Terrenos de Chavimochic.

She is a successful businesswoman and a leader in the field of women's empowerment. She has received several awards, including being recognized as one of the 15 most important Peruvian women and among the 50 most respected Peruvian business leaders. She was selected as the EY Entrepreneur Of The Year 2014 Peru winner, and represented Peru at the EY World Entrepreneur Of The Year in Monaco in 2015. Additionally, she served on the EY World Entrepreneur Of The Year independent judging panel in 2016, 2017, and 2018. She also received the Peruvian Labor Order Award for her contribution to the development of working conditions and an award from IPAE Prize – the highest distinction awarded to business leaders – for her positive impact on entrepreneurial and educational development in Peru.

DanPer occupies the first position in the MERCO Ranking for the fourth consecutive year, positioning it as a benchmark for excellence in the agribusiness, chosen in this sector as one of the best companies to work for.

* * *

As Rosario herself, the mother of two children, puts it: "More than 20 years ago, when we launched DanPer, the term 'social responsibility' had yet to be coined. But we already understood that respecting and treating our stakeholders well; promoting their development; being fair to our workers, clients, and suppliers; and looking after the environment were fundamental to making our company sustainably profitable." Also: "I have always had a firm belief that building our company while generating a permanent development dynamic is the best way we can contribute to building up our nation."

LINDA HASENFRATZ
LINAMAR GROUP
EY ENTREPRENEUR
OF THE YEAR 2014
CANADA

After taking over the reins of automotive parts manufacturing business Linamar from her father, who founded the company, Linda Hasenfratz set a bold goal to increase revenue from C$1.4 billion to C$10 billion by diversifying her product offerings and customer base through strategic acquisitions and international expansion. Today Linamar operates more than 60 plants in 17 countries – all while ensuring returns for stakeholders and developing its people.

Growing up as one of two daughters, Linda says she was shaped by her parents' values of hard work, respect for others, the value of money and the importance of spending it wisely, and a passion for innovation in business.

As a young student, Linda's favorite subjects were physics, chemistry, and math. She took calculus at the university level simply because she enjoyed it. But there was no direct path to the C-suite, even though she was equipped with a bachelor's degree (and later an MBA) from the University of Western Ontario – and she was the boss's daughter.

Linda started at Linamar in the 1990s as a machine operator. She knew that to deeply understand the business and to earn the respect of the employees, she needed to learn it from the ground up. Spending time in every area of the company – the shop floor, engineering, production control, quality assurance, accounting, and estimating – gave her invaluable experience for when she stepped into the COO's chair in 1997.

When Linda became CEO in 2002, she set a bold and aggressive financial target – C$10 billion in sales by 2020. It was a big ask for Linamar Group, the company her father, Frank Hasenfratz, a Hungarian immigrant, set up as a one-man tool shop in 1964. At the time Linda took charge, net earnings for the Ontario-based company were C$57 million on sales of C$1.4 billion. Linamar was then hit hard by the global financial crisis of 2008 and 2009, when revenue plunged by 26%, from C$2.3 billion to C$1.6 billion. Two of its major customers, General Motors and Chrysler, filed for bankruptcy; together, they accounted for nearly 25% of Linamar's sales. Its share price fell to C$3.50 in December 2009, down from C$21 a year earlier.[1]

But since 2009 the company has been on a roll and Linda is still optimistic Linamar will hit that C$10 billion sales figure. "We had a little setback," she says, "but that's still our target."

Frank attributes much of the recent success of Linamar to Linda's push to expand internationally, her financial acumen, her formal education, and her "personality plus." In an interview quoted in the Gustavson Business School blog he said, "The truth is, I could not have brought the company to where it is today."[2]

[1,2] "Recognizing an Entrepreneurial Superhero," Linda Hasenfratz, *The Peter B. Gustavson School of Business Blog*, September 13, 2016.

Linda has a strong focus on **people, behaviors, and culture** at Linamar. The leadership training she received had such a profound effect on her that she created the Linamar Entrepreneurial Advancement Program (LEAP) training program for senior executives, based on her own learning process. She and her team select young high-potential talent from every area of their business and they "LEAP" from one discipline to another, including internationally. After three or four years these people are ready to become managers in the organization and ultimately general managers of facilities.

Linda firmly believes that developing an effective strategy first requires a clear vision of who you are and where you are going.

One of the first tasks she took on as COO was shaping the corporate **culture**. She wanted to lead and formalize it into a vision that could be communicated as the company grew. The team identified a series of six core values – balance, entrepreneurship, respect, responsiveness, innovation, and hard work. They then set a goal of becoming the company of choice for key stakeholders and that's when the C$10 billion sales target was set. They later established additional goals of achieving double-digit growth annually with minimum 10% operating margins. Consistent, sustainable, profitable growth is her ultimate goal for the company.

Another key element of defining the company's culture was identifying the type of leaders Linamar wants to run its businesses: leaders with passion who are also good planners and good decision makers and communicators who can execute on their plans and who care about their employees. A belief that **culture** matters, and ensuring it is kept front and center, is an integral part of who Linda is.

Transactions and alliances are also part of Linamar's commitment to investing in the latest available technologies – for example, the Linamar purchase of McLaren Engineering in 2003. The company, founded by New Zealand motor racing hero the late Bruce McLaren, provides engineering, testing, and prototype capabilities for product and manufacturing, and has become the basis for Linamar's technical advancement.

Several years of double-digit growth have pushed revenue to C$6 billion, with profits of C$522 million. Linda has added roughly three factories annually and Linamar now has 59 plants in 17 countries across Asia, North America, and Europe employing 26,000 people. Under her control the group has become multifaceted, manufacturing parts for everything from commercial and passenger vehicles to mining, agriculture, and construction equipment.

Linda's mantra: "Don't be afraid to give it a try because you miss 100% of the shots you don't take."

As Linamar's growth has skyrocketed, so too has Linda's personal global influence. As far back as 2002 she was named as one of Canada's top 40 under 40. Since then she has become a prominent figure in discussions around international trade and the advancement of women in business. She was at the White House when Donald and Ivanka Trump met Justin Trudeau and is a key voice in the renegotiation of the North American Free Trade Agreement (NAFTA). In addition to being selected as the EY Entrepreneur Of The Year 2014 Canada, she chairs the Business Council of Canada – a nonprofit, nonpartisan organization of 150 chief executives who help make public policy.

* * *

While assuming leadership of Linamar, she had the first two of her four children and completed her MBA. Even today there are few senior female executives in the automotive industry. Commenting on the challenge of being a high-flying woman in a male-dominated field, Linda talks of "choosing not to dial into the negative frequencies." As she puts it: "There will always be negative people with preconceptions and if you look for them, you will find them. So, don't look for them. Do the job and show what you can do, and preconceptions are quickly forgotten. Let great performance do the talking, not naysayers."

Being a mother of four children is something Linda has taken in her stride, saying she and her husband, New Zealander Ed Newton, decided early on that despite their demanding careers they wanted a big family. Believing you can always find time to do the things you want to do, she says "live every moment of your life, squeeze it in. Life is too short not to, and in the end, you run out of time."

Linda has been described as an entrepreneurial super hero-ine. Her daughter Emily agrees, saying "some people say women can't do it all. I say they are wrong; my mother does do it all."

**DR. MARY LYNNE HEDLEY
AND LONNIE MOULDER**
COFOUNDERS –
TESARO, INC.
EY ENTREPRENEUR OF
THE YEAR 2017
UNITED STATES

As a result of the vision and drive of Dr. Mary Lynne Hedley and Lonnie Moulder, cofounders of biotech company TESARO, Inc., women with ovarian cancer and all cancer patients suffering from nausea through their treatments have more hope.

Mary Lynne's mother was a scientist, an unusual profession for a woman in those times. Together with her husband she taught their five children that life would be tough, with many barriers to success, but that none were insurmountable. They would need to figure it out for themselves but, if they did, they could achieve whatever they wanted. Even though Mary Lynne's father wanted her to be a lawyer, he was confident that as long as she was doing something meaningful, she would find the inspiration to succeed. Mary Lynne believes that early lesson is the key to TESARO's success. "It's the inspiration, it's a sense of meaning behind the work that we're doing which has enabled us to overcome unbelievable obstacles to get our drugs to patients."

After completing a Bachelor of Science degree in micro-biology at Purdue University, obtaining a doctoral degree in immunology from the University of Texas, and two postdoctoral fellowships at Harvard University, Mary Lynne started applying her significant scientific expertise and entrepreneurial skills to cofounding Zycos, a biotechnology company focused on immunotherapy drugs for treating cancer and viral mediated diseases.

Lonnie Moulder needed to fund his college tuition and managed to find work in the steel factory where his father was factory foreman. Working closely with his father, Lonnie learned how to manage teams and direct people. His father had a "unique way about himself" and formed a personal connection with the men in his team. Watching his father at work, Lonnie says, laid a foundation and, as he moved through his management career and gained more responsibility, it gave him insight into what it means to "manage and lead people in a real humanistic manner."

Lonnie earned a Bachelor of Science degree from Temple University and a Master of Business Administration from the University of Chicago, then worked for large pharmaceutical companies for the first 17 years of his career. These companies went from sales of US$100 million to $1 billion in revenue and, after a series of mergers, became a large international company. During this time Lonnie honed his business skills. "There is something about being in a larger company with financial discipline that has to be applied to the business fundamentals of commercialization and the chaos of innovation. You get to see and learn a lot." But as the company grew larger, he began to feel disconnected from the leadership and, eventually, from the end users, the patients.

Ultimately Lonnie became president and CEO of MGI Pharma.

The two leaders converged when MGI Pharma acquired Zycos in 2004. During their time at MGI Pharma, Lonnie and Mary Lynne collaborated in the clinical development and commercialization of several cancer therapeutics and oncology supportive care products, including Aloxi for preventing chemotherapy-induced nausea and vomiting and Dacogen for treating a type of blood cancer.

Mary Lynne and Lonnie realized they shared a deep passion for patient well-being and an understanding of how a commercial biopharma company could significantly impact the lives of individual patients and their families. This passion for the patient/customer was the key driver in motivating Lonnie and Mary Lynne to start TESARO (meaning "hidden treasure") in 2010.

The two founders shared a vision to create a biotech company totally focused on the **patient** and with a nonnegotiable set of values centered around setting audacious goals, sustainability and scalability, appreciating diversity of perspective, and an understanding that employees have lives outside work that need support and flexibility.

Due to their single-minded focus on the patient, TESARO has a sense of urgency often lost in big pharma companies. As Mary Lynne puts it: "In large organizations, something happens when you get to a particular size. All of the liabilities become more driving and change behaviors and processes and systems are introduced to protect the company and its shareholders as opposed to the primary focus being on doing the right thing for the patient." Lonnie and Mary Lynne believe it's their sense of urgency and passion to do something meaningful that is the primary driver, keeping them close to the end game and allowing them to do some amazing things in a relatively short time.

Attracting a talented team of scientists in a highly competitive market and ensuring they can understand and contribute to the science as well as the mission is integral for Mary Lynne and Lonnie. "From a **people, behaviors, and culture** perspective, it has always been about transparency," Mary Lynne says. "When people first come to work here, we share with them that it's all about the patient. When we first started the company a lot of people had a view that a biotech company could make a lot of money, but most of them fail. So, we tell people not to come here with that attitude. For us, it's all about the patients and trying to do something meaningful for the patient. We say, 'by the way, this will be the hardest thing you have ever done but if, at the end of the day, we are successful in doing this, look what we will accomplish.' We show them the impacts we have had on patients so far. We tell them about our values and try to incorporate questions into our interview process that will assess whether or not these values will be important to them. We tell them, 'we are not here to do anything little, we're doing something radically different and we're going to do something impactful' and we ask, 'are you on board with that?' "

In 2015, TESARO developed and commercialized oral VARUBI to treat chemotherapy-induced nausea and vomiting, and by 2017 it had been approved for use both in the United States and Europe. During 2012 Lonnie and Mary Lynne identified their second product candidate, ZEJULA, an anti-cancer agent with a mechanism known as PARP inhibition. Due to their professional reputations and the high-quality relationships they had built up over years, they were able to obtain ZEJULA from Merck during the first stage of human testing, despite being much smaller than many other companies vying for this product. Merck believed TESARO could advance the development and commercialization more quickly than anyone else.

There were no existing PARP inhibitors commercially available, although other companies had been developing and studying them without success. Lonnie and Mary Lynne followed the science, believing they could effectively develop ZEJULA first for the maintenance treatment of ovarian cancer and then potentially for breast, lung, and other cancers.

In March 2017, TESARO received accelerated FDA approval for ZEJULA for the maintenance treatment of women with recurrent epithelial ovarian, fallopian tube, or primary peritoneal cancer, based on unprecedented results from its uniquely designed and rapidly executed phase 3 clinical study. By November of that year, ZEJULA was approved by the European Commission for commercial sale. In less than a year, more than 2,000 doctors had prescribed this drug to 4,000 patients, generating more than US$108 million in revenue. Analysts predict sales of ZEJULA alone will peak at more than US$2 billion per year.

Lonnie and Mary Lynne's track record and ability to build relationships, raise significant capital, acquire important science and meaningful product candidates, and attract tremendously talented people to their team has made TESARO one of the world's fastest-growing biopharma companies.

Based on their strong track record, they secured significant private equity funding. The belief these early investors showed in the company has been well rewarded; TESARO's market capitalization today tops US$3 billion.

TESARO's founders are now on track to provide proven drugs that offer a better quality of life and, in the case of ovarian cancer, considerably extending patients' lives, while giving hope where previously there was none. Mary Lynne and Lonnie are emphatic that the patient has to be number one. In addition to being recognized as EY Entrepreneur Of The Year 2017 winners for the United States, Mary Lynne and Lonnie sit on a number of boards and committees, including Lonnie's role on Biotech Innovation Organization (BIO) – a leading industry organization. Both are also actively involved with their alma maters.

* * *

When Mary Lynne and Lonnie, the founders of oncology-focused biopharmaceutical company TESARO, represented the United States at the EY World Entrepreneur Of The Year 2018 competition in Monte Carlo, they stood in line with other country winners to be introduced to His Serene Highness Prince Albert II of Monaco. After the obligatory handshake and photo opportunity, the prince's reception line dispersed. In its place another line formed, as news circulated that Mary Lynne and Lonnie might have found a cure for some forms of cancer: It seemed that everyone had a family member or friend who needed the latest cutting-edge technology in cancer treatment.

The distance Mary Lynne and Lonnie traveled to attend that Monte Carlo reception was not just geographic. Eight years earlier their treasure, TESARO, didn't exist; 800 of their current staff were working elsewhere; chemotherapy-induced nausea and vomiting were being endured by patients who were already at the lowest ebb of their lives; and women being diagnosed with end-stage ovarian cancer were given little hope.

TESARO is "a company in a hurry" and every second of every hour of every day, Lonnie, Mary Lynne, and their 800 staff are driven by the mantra: "Our patients are waiting."

**RUBENS MENIN TEIXEIRA
DE SOUZA**
MRV ENGENHARIA
EY WORLD ENTREPRENEUR
OF THE YEAR 2018
BRAZIL

In June 2018, the EY World Entrepreneur Of The Year independent judging panel awarded Rubens the coveted title of EY World Entrepreneur Of The Year award. Judging by the flag waving and cheering in the ballroom, he was a very popular choice.

Within minutes of his win being announced he was asked by the *Financial Times* (*FT*) what this award meant to him. Being the humble man he is, he immediately turned the attention from himself to his mission, telling the *FT* that "my plan is to change the world for better. My company is expanding to the United States; I believe you have to be a global player and I want to make affordable homes for every person in the world." A big goal, but if past performance is an indicator of future success, he might just succeed.

Rubens created MRV, which is Latin America's largest home building company, literally from the ground up. As the son of high school sweethearts, who were studying engineering, and the grandson of an engineer who built dams and small hydro power plants, Rubens had engineering in his blood. His mother was just the third person to become an engineer in the Brazilian state of Minas Gerais.

The Menin family history had a strong influence on his education and, consequently, his future as an entrepreneur. Rubens says, "I was trained from the beginning to become an engineer. Engineering was always part of my life. As a small child I remember lessons from my mother in how to calculate and my father would take me on visits to construction sites." In addition to his love of engineering, Rubens inherited from his parents an appreciation of hard work – something he insisted on handing down to his children, who are now key personnel in the company.

Rubens's entrepreneurial life began early. At 12, he shined shoes; washed cars; and sold soccer lottery tickets (one of the main passions of this devoted fan of Clube Atletico Mineiro) to his neighbors and acquaintances. According to his father, when Rubens was 10 he already wanted to invest in the stock exchange.

As Rubens grew older, he attended a public high school and then became a student at Universidade Federal de Minas Gerais. Even before his graduation, he identified an opportunity not only to make some money, but also to begin pursuing his personal dream of building a fairer socially inclusive country through the construction of a low-cost house. Without any money, Rubens did what many first time entrepreneurs do: he asked his father, Geraldo, for some help. Understandably, his father was not sure whether the project would be finished within the proposed budget, so he made a bet with Rubens – and Rubens won. Not only was the house built for half the initial budget, but the revenue from its sale was also used in the construction of three new low-income houses based on the same model.

The first of many bricks was laid in what would begin making Rubens's entrepreneurial dream a reality – which would not only change his life but the lives of thousands of Brazilians. The proceeds from the three houses allowed the purchase of two lots for the development of 10 other houses in the outskirts of Belo Horizonte. Then in 1979 Rubens formed a partnership with his cousin Mario Menin and together they would go on to transform Brazil's real estate industry. Rubens is passionate about the positive impact of home ownership, saying, "Families who own their own homes have more dignity and can pursue new dreams."

The search for innovation has always been an obsession for Rubens. Since the first days of MRV, he sought to offer his **customers**, including low-income families, a product that would not only be affordable, but also exceed their expectations, set market trends, and establish innovative parameters. To provide security for the new homeowners, he constructed guardhouses at the gate, and to ensure a new way of life for the residents, he included landscaping and leisure areas, such as gourmet lounges, gyms, and swimming pools.

His other passion is sustainability. MRV is investing more than US$246 million in the next five years in what will be the biggest solar power project of any private Brazilian company. Rubens says, "This represents a means of democratizing energy generation and will help the electricity sector as a whole. I feel great pride that MRV is contributing sustainable solutions to my country."

Doing good, by being good, takes on a whole new meaning when you look at the revenue and profit growth that Rubens's model has produced. In 2007, the company's net revenue was US$105 million, with a net income of $13 million. To obtain

funding and finance for their rapid growth, MRV went public that year, raising US$363 million, multiplying the company's production potential and professionalizing its management. The average number of housing units built per year soared from 4,000 in 2007 to 40,000 in 2017.

Rubens's search for business efficiency and longevity was accompanied by his passion for sustainability. MRV is the only builder to be part of the Brazil Corporate Sustainability Index (ISE) portfolio. The companies listed in the ISE are noted for their corporate governance, good social and environmental practices, and sustainability of their businesses and products. In addition, MRV is the only company on the list to offset 10% of its greenhouse gas emissions through the Friend of the Climate program as well as the only one to have reached the goal of 1 million planted trees, extracting 550,000 tons of carbon dioxide from the atmosphere.

MRV is now Latin America's largest residential real estate developer and Brazil's leading low-income housing builder. MRV has enabled countless Brazilian families to take their first step on the property ladder.

The process of "industrialized construction" now allows MRV to deliver the keys to a new apartment to a family in Brazil every two-and-a-half minutes, but that's not the only impressive figure. With an average of 18,000 employees on construction sites, the company has delivered more than 320,000 houses and apartments in Brazil through 2017, allowing 1 million people to realize their home ownership dream. "As soon as a family becomes a homeowner, it changes perspective. Someone who leaves the favela and moves to their own home is able to raise their children under decent conditions," says Rubens.

Over the next 10 years, the company expects to build 500,000 homes. The amount invested should generate US$12 billion.

With this investment, MRV believes it will become the world's second largest homebuilder. Today, the real estate developer from Minas Gerais is the third largest builder in the global real estate market, after one company in China and one in the United States.

In addition to being selected as the EY World Entrepreneur Of The Year 2018, Rubens serves as president of the Brazilian Real Estate Developer Association and is a vocal advocate for home building.

* * *

Rubens's passion for seeking a fairer and more egalitarian society began a long time ago: For more than 30 years, he has invested substantial time and financial resources across Brazil. Since the beginning of MRV, he has contributed to projects such as City of Kids. This project, which is very close to his heart, provides education, sports, leisure, and culture for more than 4,000 disadvantaged children. In 2011, he created a program for 3,800 of his staff to teach them to read and write and receive professional training to become plasterers, painters, or ceramic tile layers. In 2014, MRV decided to allocate 1% of the company's annual net income to support educational projects – and in a little over three years the institute has already helped more than 219,000 children and teenagers.

Another of Rubens's passions is sport. The company's first sponsorship was offered to a volleyball team in 1994. Since then the company has supported various sports, including soccer, tennis, car racing, and martial arts. Today, it supports large Brazilian soccer teams, such as Sao Paulo Futebol, Clube Atletico Mineiro, and Flamengo, making MRV the private company that invests the most in sponsorship of teams and athletes in Brazil.

Rubens Menin's dreaming spirit and practical soul have redesigned urbanization in Brazil. The "house as the home" has always been fundamental to his character. It was in his family home that he developed a taste for simplicity and learned to appreciate people, be organized, be fair, and be plain – simple values that have underscored his leadership style. What gives him the most pleasure at MRV is to know that MRV is a people company. He says simply, "I like people."

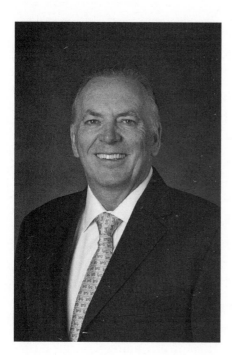

JIM NIXON
NIXON ENERGY
INVESTMENTS
EY ENTREPRENEUR OF
THE YEAR 2010 UNITED
STATES – MANUFACTURING
& DISTRIBUTION AWARD
WINNER SOUTHWEST
REGION
EY WORLD ENTREPRENEUR
OF THE YEAR JUDGE 2016,
CHAIR 2017–2018
UNITED STATES

Jim Nixon built Varel International into a market-leading company selling innovative, specialized equipment to the oil and gas industry. When Varel was acquired by Sandvik AB (Sandvik), Jim remained with Sandvik for a period of time before leaving to found Nixon Energy Investments, which continues to invest in and advise energy equipment and services businesses with high-growth potential.

How does the eighth child of a Glasgow butcher, who left school with no formal qualifications, become a world-renowned expert on manufacturing select equipment for the oil and gas market, owning a fleet of luxury cars, homes all over the world, and a private jet – and be chairman of the judging panel for the EY World Entrepreneur Of The Year? The answer from Jim is simple, "I followed my dreams, never ever gave up, and if there was a roadblock or my first idea wasn't right then I found another way and I just kept going for it. There is nothing sadder in life than the regret of not trying."

Jim's entrepreneurial journey started at the age of 10 when he bought a paper route. The lessons about cash flow, responsibility, and margins have stayed with him for all his life. Early on in his career he worked for a large corporation, and despite always having a hankering to do something more and be self-employed, the corporate world would be his home for many years.

A big influence in Jim's early life was his father, who instilled an incredible work ethic in all his children by working 12 hours a day, 6 days a week. Nixon senior, a butcher, was very determined that each of his children would learn a trade. His best piece of advice: "Not everybody is going to be great on a team, you just have to find out what they are good at and help them be better." This became Jim's mantra, enabling him to manage large numbers of people and grow internationally renowned teams. Jim was only 10 when his father died, and he then looked to his seven brothers and sisters for advice and inspiration. They remind him now that even as a small child he was incredibly fascinated by how things worked and that he had a natural mechanical aptitude. His mother, too, was very supportive of his need to "tinker with stuff," allowing him to work on his first motorcycle (which he bought at 13) inside the house. From his family, Jim absorbed a hunger to do better and achieve more, with a desire to deliver more for his own children. Now when he looks for staff, he wants to see that they have the same passion and hunger, saying, "We can teach technical skills, but we can't teach passion, and we can't make people hungry for success."

At 16 Jim left school, deciding college was not for him. He was offered three or four apprenticeships. He decided to work for Weir Pumps where he got "fantastic technical training on the job for four years" – learning everything from production, assembly, and milling, to how to work with people. But halfway through he realized that he had made a mistake in not seeking higher education, so while continuing to work full-time he earned associate degrees in mechanical engineering and in production engineering, eventually becoming a service and commissioning engineer.

For four or five years he worked all over the world on power stations, submarines, and oil tankers. Eventually the head office realized that everywhere he went they got follow-up business, so Jim was moved into general management. Very soon he became the managing director of a North Sea group of companies and then was offered a role in Dallas, Texas, as senior vice president of a large division, with a group of companies reporting to him. Jim made the move to Texas to be groomed to become the division president.

Despite his rapid climb up the corporate ladder, Jim had a hankering to own his own business and finally decided to "take control of my own destiny." He bought a small family business and put together a team of people from his corporate world, found some investors, and Varel International Energy Services was born. "We took a lot of time with a lot of great people and eventually we established an outstanding manufacturing base." His vision was to take this business to US$1 billion of sales. Not only did he almost reach his goal but, over the years, he has managed to buy and sell the same business three times, through participation in two separate private equity transactions and the ultimate sale to Sandvik.

Jim has had a strong focus on **people, behaviors, and culture** and on technology and creating a culture of continuous innovation to attract and retain **customers**. When Jim bought Varel they had sales of US$40 million. He set out to be the preferred supplier for the blue-chip oil and gas market. When he communicated this to his staff along with his dream to take revenues to US$100 million there was incredulous laughter. Three years later with sales at US$250 million, the laughing had stopped because everyone was committed to hitting the next goal of being a US$1 billion company. According to Jim, this phenomenal growth occurred because he encouraged the staff, listened to their ideas, and engaged them in the process of continuous improvement across every aspect of the business. "Once you have success in one area you can push that through into every aspect of the business," Jim says. Jim passionately believes in incentives as the key motivator for achieving buy-in from all levels of employees, so when he wanted to create a lean enterprise environment everybody was on board and success was inevitable.

Having sold Varel, Jim established Nixon Energy Investments to invest in and advise energy equipment and service businesses with high-growth potential. Jim is now the chairman of three companies, on the board of two others, and has "skin in the game" in them all. His primary objective is to coach and mentor the CEOs to help them replicate the sort of success that he has created with his past companies.

In addition to being selected as EY Entrepreneur Of The Year 2010 United States category winner, and in recognition of his personal entrepreneurial achievements, his leadership abilities, and his commitment to entrepreneurship, Jim has served on the EY World Entrepreneur Of The Year independent judge's panel for 2016–2018, the latter two years as chair.

* * *

Jim's wife of 43 years, Caroline, an entrepreneur in her own right, has been with him through the entire journey, offering support and advice and pushing him to do more. She is a partner in evaluating investment risk and fully supportive. Dubbed by one director as the "She-E-O," she has always been interested and engaged in the business.

Entrepreneurs based in Asia Pacific

CRAIG HEATLEY
FOUNDER – RAINBOW
CORPORATION AND
SKY TV
EY ENTREPRENEUR OF
THE YEAR 2012
NEW ZEALAND

Craig Heatley is an icon of New Zealand business. From humble beginnings, he created two of New Zealand's most successful publicly listed companies. In the early 1980s he founded Rainbow Corporation – a leisure, entertainment, and retail business – and a year later, created SKY TV – one of the most successful start-up businesses in the history of New Zealand.

Today he is a committed philanthropist, jet pilot, and international investor, but the role he enjoys most is Dad to his four children.

At the age of 11, Craig started delivering the morning news-paper in a town where the winter morning temperature was rarely above zero. On Thursdays, he would receive a little brown enve-lope containing just over NZ$2. He added to the contents of the brown envelopes by cleaning cars and filling coal sacks with pine cones that he sold around the neighborhood. His father died when he was 13, and this left a huge gap in his family. He felt an over-whelming sense of responsibility for his mother and younger sister.

He hadn't set out to be a media magnate or global entrepreneur – he'd simply wanted more of what was in that little brown envelope. He was also studying the stock market and making some small trades. By the time he was 15, he'd saved $300 and was ready to take on the world.

Property was his first move. He managed to get the vendor of 10 acres of residentially zoned land to sell it to him. The man wanted $10,000; Craig offered him the full price, with one condition: He'd get paid when Craig subdivided and collected deposits on the sites. The deal saw Craig turn $300 into $17,000. He was 17 and still in school uniform.

After attending university, he got a job he hated with a big com-pany. Then came the light-bulb moment that became Rainbow Cor-poration. At the age of 23, Craig saw an opportunity, took a chance, and walked away from his job and company car. "I knew I wasn't cut out to be an employee. I don't mean this in a negative way, but I found it claustrophobic and I didn't like having controls put on me."

He sank everything he had, including his own labor and blisters, into a miniature golf course in Taupo, a small lakefront holiday village on the North Island of New Zealand. Craig had NZ$3,000, his business partner had NZ$5,000, but they needed NZ$40,000 to build it.

The land they wanted was leasehold and they needed to cover it with concrete. The bank refused to lend to them because they had no security. Craig did, however, charm his bank manager into a NZ$5,000 personal loan. They opened accounts with local suppliers (no one ever asked if they had any money). They had to employ one person, a builder, because they had no idea how much reinforcing to put into concrete. Then they took to wheelbarrows and built it themselves. It took four months.

"We opened at Easter, the beginning of winter in New Zealand. We got four fine days. Taupo hasn't had four fine days at Easter in the almost 30 years since. We took NZ$16,000 in four days. That validated the business. If it had rained, I wouldn't be sitting here today because we'd have gone broke."

From hand-building his miniature golf course, it took Craig only two years to take Rainbow Corporation from nothing to a company poised for international corporate stardom.

At its heart was the theme park, Rainbow's End, which has since become an Auckland institution. But in 1981, it was still an idea in Craig's head when he and his partner went calling on banks.

"Here we were, trying to borrow more than NZ$1 million at 14% interest and our only security was a leisure park that did not exist, on land we did not own."

In 1984, he floated Rainbow Corporation. People said he was prescient because he did it just before the incoming Labor government deregulated the financial and investment environment, sending the stock market into a frenzy.

"I'd like to say I saw that coming, but I didn't. That was luck!" He says he's always been driven, inspired, and astute, but also been lucky. "Luck plays a big part in life, in my opinion, a much bigger part than a lot of us think." That luck often seemed to come on the back of vision, risk, nerve, charm, and an awful lot of hard work.

At the time of the float, the business had a market capitalization of $6 million. Three years later it had grown to $600 million, an annual growth rate of 364%.

At its peak, Rainbow was subject to a takeover by Brierley Investments, just three months before the 1987 stock market crash. When that happened, Craig's selling of Rainbow appeared to show great foresight. As a friend pointed out, if he'd stayed five more minutes, he would have crawled out on his belly.

"He thought I must have had some presentiment of the crash. The truth is, I was a reluctant bridesmaid for Brierley. I didn't want that takeover. Once again I was lucky."

The next journey Craig's heart was to take him on was an even bigger roller coaster ride.

"Light-bulb moments happen rarely but when they do, they change the direction of your life. Rainbow was one of those pivotal points. SKY TV was another."

Cashed-up and bored with retirement, he was ready for a new challenge when a colleague walked through the door with an idea. A lifelong poker player, Craig doesn't consider himself a gambler, but the idea of bringing horse racing live to New Zealand from Australia seemed pretty good.

That quickly morphed into pay-for-view television, which went from an interesting business that might go to a hundred bars and clubs to a much more ambitious product that might be sold in every home in New Zealand.

"In those days, we only had one state-owned TV channel in New Zealand and most people couldn't understand the need for more. Why would anyone pay for something they were currently getting for nothing?"

Craig acknowledged that he didn't know anything about the media industry so the new company, SKY TV, went looking for people with specific media knowledge and for a shareholder who knew the business and could open doors. Kerry Packer's Channel 9 seemed to fit the bill; they shook hands on a deal where Packer's Consolidated Press would buy 20% of SKY for NZ$2.8 million (currently about US$1.9 million), but the deal collapsed within weeks.

"There was a time in 1991 where we were losing a million dollars a week. I promise you that gets your attention when it's coming straight out of your pocket. My investors, who had invested anticipating fun and profit, were getting neither. They were loyal but sick of it." To improve operations and stem these losses, SKY TV sold half the business to four giant U.S. companies (Time Warner, TCI, Ameritech, and Bell Atlantic) for US$108 million. That deal was the turning point.

Who was the loser? SKY TV went on to become New Zealand's most successful start-up and is one of New Zealand's top 10 public companies. That 20% is now worth NZ$600 million or more.

Craig has always focused on the importance of **people, behaviors, and culture**. Getting the right team around him is crucial for Craig – he doesn't have to be the most clever person in the room (although he usually is). He is comfortable having smarter people around him; he wants people to challenge him and likes to thrash things out amongst a group of people he trusts.

He seeks out staff and colleagues with skills complementary to his own because he knows his own weaknesses. "I am the world's worst administrator, for instance. If I have a strength, it's probably the big picture – the tectonic plates as opposed to the grains of sand," he says.

He wants his team to feel empowered and to feel a valued part of something bigger, because, as he says, a good team will outperform several smart individuals every day.

In addition to a strong team, Craig accelerated the growth of SKY TV through **transactions and alliances** – strategic relationships that also brought capital.

The other key growth driver was a good understanding of the **customer** and his or her needs – in particular, quality programming. Craig built a strong relationship with ESPN through sheer perseverance, his premise being that if he could secure programming from them, others would have the confidence to follow.

He offered ESPN a small share in SKY TV, which it eventually accepted. That had a domino effect, with CNN following soon after, and film studios after that. Then, in 1996, rugby became a professional international sport and SKY TV was able to do a deal with Rupert Murdoch for exclusive coverage. In rugby-mad New Zealand, that guaranteed SKY TV a subscriber base.

Looking back at that battle for viability, Craig can extract several lessons:

- Don't get too optimistic on the revenue and be very pessimistic on the costs.
- Never underestimate the competitive response.
- Always ask yourself, "What is the worst possible thing that could happen to my business?" Proceed only if you are sure you can live with the downside of what you are contemplating.

Today SKY TV is a household brand in New Zealand, viewed in 50% of New Zealand homes. It employs almost 1,000 people, has a market capitalization of NZ$2 billion, and an EBITDA of NZ$320 million.

Craig had again simply been following his dream. He was proven right, but it was a narrow squeak. One investor, Alan Gibbs, described it as "probably the scariest ride I've ever had." This from the man who developed the world's first commercial amphibious car.

In addition to being named the EY Entrepreneur Of The Year 2012 New Zealand, the queen made Craig a Companion of the New Zealand Order of Merit in 2013 for his services to business.

* * *

For the past 10 years, more than a third of Craig's time has been spent on not-for-profit and charitable activities.

His love of golf has taken him to the almost sacred green sward of Augusta National, where he's a member of the executive committee and chairman of the Masters Tournament media committee. It's also taken him to two titles, the 2003 AT&T Pebble Beach National Pro-Am at Pebble Beach with professional golfer Phil Tataurangi, and the 2004 Alfred Dunhill Links Championship pro-am with professional golfer Fred Couples.

His other great love is flight, although he says it's accidental that his two largest businesses were called Rainbow Corporation and SKY TV.

When pressed on what advice he would give his children if they were starting their own businesses, he said, "A good idea helps, you must be prepared to back yourself and you must be prepared to give up other things if you really want your idea to work. Honesty and integrity are really important but drive and an ability to change as you go and be adaptable are essential.

"Someone wise once said, success is getting what you want: Happiness is enjoying what you've got. These days, I enjoy what I've got."

OLIVIA LUM
HYFLUX LTD.
EY WORLD ENTREPRENEUR
OF THE YEAR 2011
SINGAPORE

Olivia, who lived her early life in poverty, dared to leave a promising career at Glaxo Pharmaceuticals to leverage an emerging water purification membrane technology and create Hyflux Ltd. Her focus on exploiting new technologies, making the most of University alliances, and delivering real value to customers established her capabilities in building and operating large desalination plants in Asia, Africa, and the Middle East.

Without water, there is no life. With water, Olivia Lum, through her business Hyflux Ltd., has transformed not only her life but the lives of millions of people across the globe who, thanks to Olivia's perseverance, passion, and persistence, now have access to clean drinking water.

Olivia, a Singaporean entrepreneur, was awarded EY World Entrepreneur Of The Year in 2011. Her rags-to-Prada story captured not only the hearts of the independent judging panel but the science behind her work captured their minds as well.

Water has always played a central role in Olivia's life. Abandoned as a newborn baby and adopted by an elderly woman she called "Grandmother," Olivia joined a family of four nonbiological siblings. Unfortunately, Grandmother was a gambler, and by the time Olivia was three, Grandmother had gambled away their modest home playing Mahjong. The family was forced to move to a tin shack with no electricity or running water.

Olivia has two strong memories from that shack: the stomach-churning stench of kerosene and how she would race to complete her homework in two hours because if she didn't, she had to refill the kerosene lamp; and a memory about water. Even as a young child, it was her job to carry water from a communal well to the shack. Olivia hated the fact that while carrying the bucket, the water would spill, and, despite her best efforts, there was often little left by the time she got home.

Finding enough food and water were the most important occupations for Grandmother's children. If they couldn't find a church or temple giving away free meals, they went hungry. The children would amuse themselves by running competitions to see who would be the first to return home with free food.

Not only were food and water in short supply but Olivia had only one pair of shoes. When they became too small, she had to cut off the ends, so she could wear them with her toes hanging out. When she heard that a sports shoe company was donating a pair of running shoes as a prize for a school race, she was determined to win.

Although Olivia had been barred from physical education because her malnutrition and low weight meant exercise made her ill, she trained her strength by securing bags of stones to her legs. Olivia won the race and the shoes.

As a young person, her sole focus was on earning enough money so her family could eat. She did several jobs. She made rattan bags for SGD\$1 a day. She worked as a rubber tapper, getting up at 4:00 AM to tap the rubber trees before the sun rose and the rubber hardened and stopped flowing. She foraged for fruit on her way to school and set up a stall to sell papaya. Her form teacher noticed what a good salesperson Olivia was and before long, she was working for her teacher's husband, selling jeans. She was the best salesperson he had.

Olivia says needing money to eat taught her how to be an entrepreneur. "It trains you to have discipline and how to approach customers," she says. Her strong conviction is that business and entrepreneurship have, at their heart, the ability to sell. If you put your customers' needs first and understand what they really "need" rather than what you think they "want," you will be successful, she says.

It was unusual for children raised in the sort of poverty Olivia experienced to have anything but the most basic education. Her siblings received only three years' schooling before becoming child laborers.

Olivia, however, used her selling skills to convince Grandmother to continue her schooling. Grandmother agreed, but only if Olivia was also willing to keep doing the manual jobs that supported the family. She studied chemistry at the National University of Singapore, graduating with an honors degree.

Back then, in 1986, "entrepreneurs" and "entrepreneurship" were dirty words in Singapore, but Olivia knew she wanted to sell things and build a business. Her lecturers talked her out of this and were delighted when she accepted a job at Glaxo Pharmaceutical as a chemist.

Three-and-a-half years later, having, as she puts it, "no contacts and not knowing the outside world," Olivia followed her entrepreneurial nose by selling her only assets, an apartment and a car, and raising SGD$20,000 – an act that was especially difficult for someone who had started life as an abandoned baby. After taking a lease on a small building and buying basic office equipment, this dwindled to SGD$10,000. Olivia realized her only way forward was to become an agent for a large water company.

But Singaporean businesses were not interested in purchasing water products through an agent rather than directly from the manufacturer. Instead, she bought a 100cc motorbike and, armed with a business card describing herself as a "manager," she crossed the causeway to Malaysia each day and found customers.

Olivia describes this door-knocking as "hard sell." Many times, she wanted to give up and return to the security of Glaxo, but over time, she secured a few small orders and the business grew. She was selling other people's products in Malaysia, but Olivia wanted to create and sell her own technology.

"I knew that membrane technology was the most efficient way to clean up water," she says, "and at that time, no one was in the membrane business." Recognizing the important role of **transactions and alliances**, and with the support of her university lecturers, she built a small membrane plant. The business, Hydrochem, set up in 1989 and the precursor of Hyflux, was soon recycling water in Singapore, and from there her success began to grow.

Since membranes are a scalable technology, by the time Hyflux was awarded the Singspring desalination plant project, she was in a position to prove the many doubters wrong by building the then largest membrane-based desalination plant in the world.

Olivia has also pursued various **funding and finance** options, and in 2001, Hyflux became a listed company with a SGD$7 million raised in capital. The listing took place during a financial crisis and Olivia laments that they had to sell into the market very cheaply. But she prefers to be a listed company rather than a joint venture or partnership.

Olivia describes being an entrepreneur as like climbing a mountain without luggage: In a joint venture you climb with a haversack, but in a listed company you are climbing with a trolley which you must drag behind you. This can stifle some entrepreneurs, but it was the only option for Hyflux. As Olivia puts it: "I came from nowhere and my personal resources were limited, so going public gave me a bigger base to grow from."

Hyflux has built landmark desalination plants in Asia, Africa, and the Middle East. The global water desalination market is set to reach US$26.81 billion by 2025[1] and Hyflux is well positioned to capture a large portion of this market. Being the first to see the potential of this market, Olivia has now turned her attention to the part water plays in health and beauty.

Several years ago, she began studying the parts of the world where people lived the longest. Her theory was that there was "something in the water." She visited some of these places and obtained water samples, which were analyzed in her laboratory in Singapore. The analysis showed the water in these regions was rich in oxygen content.

In the past few years, Olivia has turned her attention to producing oxygen-rich water. Today, clinical trials are taking place in Singapore and Australia that may prove her theory correct. In 2017, Monash University did a study on lab mice injected with human prostate cancer cells and discovered that the mice drinking Hyflux's ELO oxygen-rich water developed smaller cancer tumors than the control mice drinking tap water. This study was significant in proving that drinking ELO water delivered oxygen to the tissues, resulting in biological effects. With Changi General Hospital in Singapore, human clinical trials on the efficacy of ELO Drinking Water for diabetic control and diabetic foot ulcers are currently underway.

---

[1] Source: Hexa Research, cited in PRNewswire release of August 29, 2017.

It's Olivia's dream to go from being a "business-to-government" operation to being "business-to-consumer." As well as marketing her ELO water directly to consumers, she has established ELO Bath Sessions that people attend to soak in the optimized oxygen-rich water.

These baths are proving highly successful, with customers reporting everything from a cure for jet lag to shrinking skin ulcers. ELO water is also being used to make cosmetic skin products; a clinical study concluded by the Dermapro Research Institute in Seoul, South Korea, shows ELO gel improves the color, elasticity, hydration, and gloss of human skin in a short period of time.

In addition to being the first female entrepreneur to be recognized by the independent judging panel as the EY World Entrepreneur Of The Year 2011, Olivia has a number of recognitions and public service memberships to her name. She won the Global Female Invent and Innovate Award, and has served on a number of boards including SPRING, Singapore National University Singapore Council, Singapore Exchange, and UNESCAP Business Advisory Council, and is a past member of the Parliament of Singapore.

*   *   *

In an interview with *Water & Wastewater International* magazine in 2015 Olivia said: "A lot of entrepreneurs may have a great idea, good products, and good suggestions, but they give up too easily, they don't persevere enough. As an entrepreneur, perseverance is a must-have attitude. Just don't give up!"

MANNY STUL
MOOSE TOYS
EY WORLD ENTREPRENEUR
OF THE YEAR 2016
AUSTRALIA

Despite living in a refugee camp and converted army barracks when he was a very young boy, Manny Stul found his passion for children's toys late in life with Moose Toys. Moose is an Australian-based children's toy business that Manny and his team have grown – through their commitment to developing unique, innovative products – to be one of the top five toy companies in the world.

The son of two Polish Holocaust survivors, Manny was born in a refugee camp near Munich, in the palace of a former Prussian empress. The family emigrated to Australia when he was seven months old. Initially they lived in a converted army barracks in a small town north of Perth. When they moved to the city three years later, it was to a house they shared with three other families.

Watching his parents work long hours in factories fueled Manny's entrepreneurial drive. His parents wanted him to be a doctor or a lawyer but after leaving school he worked a variety of jobs before deciding in his early 20s that he wanted to start a business.

To get the necessary capital, Manny worked as a laborer in the extreme heat of remote northwestern Australia. His first business, Skansen, was an innovative gift company. He had no experience, training, or mentors, but starting from scratch enabled him to obtain firsthand knowledge of every component of its operations. Manny took Skansen public in 1993 in an IPO before selling his stake for AUS$17 million.

By this stage, he was ready to get out. He was finding no joy in his business, saying "The year before I sold my gift company, I had accomplished everything I wanted to do. I had this feeling of being trapped and overwhelmed, and I really didn't enjoy the last year there. It taught me a lesson – that if you are going to do anything in your life, make sure you love what you are doing, find your passion, and don't be driven by money alone." After selling the business, Manny never needed to work again. He was 41 years old.

"I didn't want to work again," he says. "And I wasn't intending to. I wanted to settle down and have an organic farm and a rural retreat."

In 2002, after a 10-year retirement, Manny and two other investors acquired Moose Toys. The business had just 10 employees and a turnover of US$4 million. Within 18 months, he had overhauled the company, bought out his coinvestors, and taken 100% control. Coping with crises and the fear of failure are "business as usual" for successful entrepreneurs. But few have been tested like Australia's Manny Stul, CEO of Moose Toys, the global company he brought back from a near-death experience in 2007, after his best-selling Bindeez toy was subject to a global recall. Manny emerged successfully, thanks in part to his focus on having great **people**, resilient **operations** and supply chain, and managing **risk** – especially from regulators.

Unbeknownst to Manny, Moose's Chinese manufacturer had replaced a nontoxic glue with something much cheaper which, when mixed with saliva, metabolized into the date-rape drug GHB (gammahydroxybutrate). Several children around the world were hospitalized after playing with the toy; Manny's advisers recommended he file for bankruptcy.

The recall disaster struck in 2007, just after the highly successful product line, Bindeez, was named Toy of the Year in Australia and the United Kingdom. Moose voluntarily arranged a global recall of Bindeez, the product that was generating nearly 90% of the company's turnover.

A potentially catastrophic chain of events was set off: Bindeez was banned and it looked as if Moose would be liable for refunds of up to 15 million units (and hundreds of millions of dollars) that had already been sold. Worse still, Moose's distributors and retailers were considering significant legal claims against the company. And the Chinese government banned Moose from exporting any of its products that had been produced in China-based factories.

Faced with enormous reputational damage and immediate solvency issues, Manny was advised to file for bankruptcy protection. But instead, he assembled a team of Moose staffers and advisers to devise a recovery plan. For 12 weeks, the team worked around the clock, trying to persuade Moose's 37 distributors not to put the company into receivership.

Manny flew to Hong Kong to meet all his stakeholders in person. The distributors had a choice: a return of 5 cents on the dollar if Moose was put into receivership or 15 cents on the dollar over three years if Manny was allowed to trade on. He managed to persuade all 37 to sign the release documentation – something his advisers said would be impossible, as it required unanimous agreement.

At the same time, Manny was working to find an alternative supplier he could trust to manufacture the reformulated product to "food grade" specification. He then persuaded the Chinese government to lift the export ban on Moose products and the Australian government to allow the reformulated product back on the market. To get these bans lifted, Manny signed personal guarantees with regulators that the revised product was fail-safe, with criminal penalties attached.

It took him nine months to finalize the negotiations, testing regimes, and regulatory undertakings. Cash flow during that period was severely negative as minimal revenue was coming in and expenses were mounting. During the crisis, not a single staff member was retrenched. By June 2008, Moose was confident it had survived against the worst possible odds.

What is Manny's magic? He says it's about finding your passion and then being driven by it. He lives every day ensuring a meaningful focus on his integrity, ethics, and honesty, and treating everyone with respect. With a business lens, it's also about thinking globally, and not giving up when confronted with adversity. Manny thrives not only on being disruptive and finding an opportunity in the market, but also ensures his decisions are not being guided only by money. His mantra is to hire the very best people and always listen and to trust his intuition.

Against the odds, he and his team pulled the company back from the brink. Today, the small Melbourne toy company he bought into in 2002 is the number five toy company in the United States, behind Mattel, Hasbro, and Lego, and its products are sold in over 100 countries.

One of the company's most successful product lines, Shopkins, has sold more than 600 million toy characters since its launch in 2014.

Moose has no debt and is still owned 100% by Manny and his family. He feels blessed that his 40-year-old stepson is a driven and talented man, so the company's succession plan is firmly in place.

In addition to being chosen as the EY World Entrepreneur Of The Year 2016 winner, Manny served as a member of the 2017 and 2018 EY World Entrepreneur Of The Year independent judging panels, in recognition of his considerable abilities as an entrepreneur.

*   *   *

As Manny told *Forbes*, "Everyone thinks we are a toy company. I keep telling our team we are not a toy company, we are a creative house, a creative hub. Innovation is in our DNA."[2]

---

[2] https://www.forbes.com/profile/manny-stul/#611bfadd1bf0

MICHAEL WU
MAXIM GROUP
EY ENTREPRENEUR OF THE
YEAR 2012
HONG KONG

When Michael Wu graduated from prestigious Brown University, he declined all the lucrative investment banking offers he received, choosing instead to return to Hong Kong and join the restaurant business his grandfather had founded in 1956.

Subsequently, Michael Wu transformed the Hong Kong based Maxim Group, which he took over from his grandfather in 2000, into Hong Kong's largest restaurant group, developing and operating its own concepts, as well as operating franchises with leading US brands such as Starbucks and Shake Shack.

Ivy League Brown University in Providence, Rhode Island, boasts many famous alumni, including the late John F. Kennedy Jr., actor Emma Watson, and CNN founder Ted Turner. Among this eminent group is one of the world's best-educated fast-food delivery boys, Michael Wu of Hong Kong.

Michael was completing his studies at Brown when his grandfather, S.T. Wu, cofounder of Hong Kong's Food and Beverage Group Maxim's, made him an offer: Instead of joining Merrill Lynch after graduation and becoming an investment banker, Michael should pull on his jeans and train as a delivery boy. His grandfather promised that if he did well, one day Michael might become the boss.

As a young boy, Michael had accompanied his grandfather to the family restaurants to taste the food, talk to the chefs, and hear S.T. Wu criticize every dish – so he knew his grandfather was a hard man to please. But he was still prepared to forego Merrill Lynch's offer of US$40,000 a year plus bonus and, armed with his degree in applied mathematics and economics, Michael returned to Hong Kong to start waiting tables and delivering frozen chicken drumsticks to his fast-food stores.

By working at the grass roots of the business, Michael says he learned how hard the restaurant staff worked and what motivated them. By doing the work himself, he came to understand the challenges and back stories of the people he would one day lead.

For example, as a young delivery boy he invited a fellow truck driver to lunch and was shocked to discover the truck driver would rather work through lunch and get home to be with his family a half an hour earlier, rather than sacrifice that half an hour for lunch. It wasn't until he became a parent himself that Michael understood how important that extra half hour was.

On another occasion, one of the kitchen staff felt sorry for the young boy carrying 20 kg bags of frozen chicken legs and offered him a piece of toast, thinking he must be hungry. Michael says it was the best piece of toast he ever had because it was hard-earned. On another occasion he was offered the leftovers from a buffet: a feast for a boy finishing a 10-hour shift as a waiter.

In 2000, when Michael was 29, his grandfather decided he was good enough to be the boss. His grandfather retired but didn't disappear. He kept a close eye on Michael and wanted to know about everything that was happening in the business. "My grandfather wanted to make decisions on everything, no matter how small," Michael says. "He was very opinionated but that was good as his judgment was usually correct."

When Michael joined in 2000, the business was well-known in Hong Kong for its cake shops, moon cakes, and dim sum. It had actually begun life in 1956 as a single western restaurant founded by S.T. Wu and his brother James, who decided to set up their own establishment because many restaurant owners at the time thought Chinese didn't order wine – weren't big spenders – so they were often seated near the toilets.

From his early experiences working his way up in the company, Michael says he learned the importance of **people, behaviors, and culture**. For Michael, this includes good communication and treating those who are the backbone of his business with respect. He has always set aside two days a week to visit stores and talk to managers, kitchen staff, crew, and even customers. "Speaking with my employees shapes some of the most important decisions I make as a leader," he says.

Michael also has an intense focus on understanding and addressing **customer** demographics and changing needs and preferences. One of Michael's first hurdles was to transform a brand established in 1956 into something attractive to a new generation of customers. Looking back at the business he "inherited," he can see its biggest challenge was its rapidly aging, 40-year-old demographic. He needed to capture a new 20- to 30-year-old market, so he created more lifestyle, youth-focused brands of his own such as Simply Life, Arome Bakery, M.C. Duck, and others. He also rejuvenated the Group's traditional formats such as Jade Garden and Maxim's Cakes, transforming them into modern dining concepts. Recently, Maxim's pioneered the "lava custard mooncake," a delicious and innovative product that still embodies the traditional spirit of Mid-Autumn Festival yet appeals to the younger Chinese consumers. The transformation journey of Maxim's continues as Michael understands the need to constantly refresh, rejuvenate, and rebrand in order to stay relevant.

Michael's decision to acquire the Starbucks franchise (despite a fierce battle with his grandfather, who preferred his regular Italian blend) has proven profitable and has opened the door to that younger customer base he was seeking. The franchise not only brought the coffee culture to Hong Kong but also transformed the way people enjoy their free time. Following the Starbucks acquisition, Maxim's has now acquired other international brands, including Shake Shack, Cheesecake Factory, and Genki Sushi. The use of these **transactions and alliances** has helped to propel the growth of Maxim's.

Company culture has always been crucial for Michael. This includes placing employees and customers first and a "laser focus" on great value for the money. "The key to a sustainable food and beverage company is good quality control. You need to build a good team to ensure good and consistent quality of products and services.

"Every entrepreneur needs to have an idea of how to make or offer something better," he says. "We launched communal dining tables at some of our new restaurants in 2000 before anybody else was doing it in Hong Kong. People said Chinese don't like to share tables and it was a bad idea, a waste of space. But I wanted to create community within our restaurants by having people share a meal over a communal table. The young people loved it."

He also took up the trend of open kitchens, where customers can see their food being made from scratch. But he also learned from his mistakes: an experiment with themed restaurants (Hello Kitty Café) was a failure.

From that single site, the business is now Hong Kong's largest restaurant group. Owned 50% by Dairy Farm International Holdings and an associate of the Jardine Matheson Group, the business is still run by the Wu family. Today they employ 32,000 people, with 1,200 outlets covering Hong Kong, Mainland China, and, increasingly, parts of Southeast Asia.[3]

Michael plans to use Maxim's existing networks and experiences in Hong Kong and Southern China to extend its presence, by attracting the best and brightest from all industries. He has a vision for Maxim's to become the best managed company in the region.

In recognition of his considerable entrepreneurial ability, Michael was recognized as the EY Entrepreneur Of The Year 2012 for Hong Kong and has served on the independent judging panel for the EY World Entrepreneur Of The Year program.

* * *

Michael continues to expand the footprint of the business that his grandfather founded and Maxim Group now serves hundreds of thousands of customers every day.

---

[3] "Maxim's Journey from Start-Up to Hong Kong's Largest Restaurant Group," *South China Morning Post*, April 27, 2016, updated May 4, 2016.

UDAY KOTAK
FOUNDER, KOTAK
MAHINDRA BANK
EY WORLD ENTREPRENEUR
OF THE YEAR 2014
INDIA

Uday Kotak, through the identification of evolving customer needs, execution of important strategic transactions, and careful management of risk, has built the fourth largest private bank in India (now known as Kotak Mahindra Bank) – with assets of more than US$31 billion, employing more than 30,000 people, and banking over 14 million customers.

Uday Kotak, the billionaire founder and Executive Vice Chairman, Managing Director, and Chief Executive Officer of Kotak Mahindra Bank, was born into an upper-middle-class joint family, with more than 60 family members living under one roof and sharing a kitchen.

The family were cotton traders and, initially, that was where Uday was also destined to work, alongside his cousins and other relatives. The setup, which he describes as "capitalism at work, socialism at home," taught him important lessons about how people tick, while the communal lifestyle reinforced the group's already strong family values.

As a young child, Uday had a strong interest in the financial services sector, devouring every piece of information he could find about Wall Street.

At the turn of this century, India was experiencing a big demographic shift. The burgeoning upper middle class was fast evolving and Uday felt the "country of savers" was transforming into a "country of spenders and investors." At the same time a huge pool of underserved middle-income customers were frustrated by the inefficient state-owned banks that controlled most of the market. At the time, private sector financial services in India were at a nascent stage of development. This presented a huge opportunity for a privately owned bank.

Seeing this opportunity, once he'd finished his MBA, Uday declined an offer from Unilever and borrowed US$250,000 from family and friends to set up a bill discounting business, Kotak Capital Management Finance Ltd. In the early 1980s, when India was a closed economy and economic growth was muted, it was unthinkable for someone from a middle-income family to refuse a lucrative corporate job, but Uday was clear about what he wanted to do.

Uday believes strong businesses are built on the backs of strong corporate and personal brands, so when he decided to set up his own business, he was clear about wanting his name on it.

The turning point came in 2003 when Uday's business was awarded the first banking licence ever given to a private financial services company in India. He obtained some early investment from Anand Mahindra and rebranded the business Kotak Mahindra Bank Ltd.

Uday has successfully focused on many growth drivers in building Kotak Mahindra Bank. He is known for spotting game-changing **transaction and alliance** opportunities, which have also enabled him to bring new products and services to existing **customers** and to expand the business to attract new customers. Believing that financial services is a reputation game, he has forged partnerships with global behemoths, thus leveraging their brands, expertise, and networks.

In 1995 he pulled off a deal that was unthinkable for a small, unknown private Indian finance company: Uday set up a joint venture with Goldman Sachs for investment banking and stock-broking. He has also extended the bank's business to the United States, United Kingdom, UAE, Singapore, and Mauritius, by targeting remittance payments from these countries.

His bank also became involved with international investment banking for Indian corporates and investment products in India for international customers. While businesses, like capital markets, are cyclical in nature, asset management provides annuity revenues that allow Kotak to benefit from shifts in fund flows in India's financial ecosystem.

If Uday has a magic formula it's about always leading from the front, having a strong and continuing purpose, executing "what is in your core," and focusing on **people, behaviors, and culture** – having people who believe in you and your philosophy. His personal mantra is, "You cannot talk; you have to work."

Worrying about his competitors is something that keeps him awake at night. But he says he has innovation running through his veins and has a penchant for thinking outside the box.

Kotak knew the bank needed to build up its deposit base to fuel its growth, while staying true to his management philosophy of keeping his strategy simple yet prudent. Being a late entrant in the banking market made this task even more challenging. After the Reserve Bank of India relinquished control of savings bank interest rates in October 2011, Kotak was the first bank to raise interest rates on savings bank deposits from 3.5% to 5.5%

and 6%. This resulted in savings bank deposit rates climbing by 2.5 times in the next two years.

In 2016, 85% of Indian currency was demonetized. Uday and his team realized this would change the way the Indian population thought about banking and immediately commissioned a team of in-house experts to devise a solution to ensure they were servicing existing customers and acquiring new ones.

The solution was a new **digital** bank that became known as 811 (named after the day demonetization occurred). This online bank, where joining up takes customers only three minutes, has been a significant success story and is adding 500,000 new customers every month.

Uday diversified into stockbroking, investment banking, car financing, life insurance, and mutual funds. The business, now called Kotak Mahindra Bank, is the second largest private bank in India by market capitalization with assets of more than $31 billion, a customer base of 14 million, and a staff of more than of 30,000.[4,5] Uday says money cannot be "the main product" of business. "It must be something that happens because we are chasing our purpose and our dreams."

In addition to being named as the EY World Entrepreneur Of The Year 2014, Uday Kotak has been described by *Forbes* magazine as one of the 40 most powerful people in the world of finance and as a "money master" with a personal net worth of US$11 billion.[6]

Uday believes having a strong and driving purpose is critical in business. He says he has enjoyed every day of the past 33 years, particularly the sense of building and creating something that will outlast him.

---

[4] www.financialexpress.com/market/kotak-mahindra-bank-topples-sbi-to-become-indias-2nd-largest-bank-by-market-cap/1134769/
[5] www.investmentbank.kotak.com/downloads/larsen-&-toubro-technology-services-limited-DRHP.pdf
[6] www.businessinsider.in/uday-kotak-is-the-only-indian-financier-inforbes-most-powerful-list/articleshow/52238490.cms.

Entrepreneurs based in the United Kingdom, Europe

MOHED ALTRAD
THE ALTRAD GROUP
EY WORLD
ENTREPRENEUR OF
THE YEAR 2015
FRANCE

M ohed's life had an inauspicious, tough beginning. But in spite of being born in the worst of conditions, through his hunger for learning, tenacity, and determination, Mohed left his native Syria for France, where he earned his PhD and is now at the helm of the Altrad Group, one of the world's leading manufacturers of scaffolding and cement mixers.

While Mohed's true age is unknown – he says he "picked a date out of a hat" (March 9, 1948), so he could celebrate his birthday each year – he knows his life won't last forever. He is now turning his focus toward succession planning, knowing that "there is one thing in life that is certain – we will disappear."

For the past 10 years he has concentrated on how the group will carry on without him. Because of this preparation, "When I disappear there will be no trouble at all." In the meantime, his experience compensates for his lack of energy as he grows older.

It is difficult to imagine a more unpromising start to life than that of Mohed Altrad. The founder and CEO of Altrad Group was born in the Syrian Desert to a 12-year-old Bedouin girl who had been raped. He doesn't know his exact date of birth, but his mother died the day he was born and Mohed was raised by his grandmother.

He was destined to become a shepherd – his grandmother believed that schooling was only for "lazy people" and forbade him to attend. He went anyway, "stealing" his education by peering through a hole in the classroom wall until a teacher finally invited him inside. He was a clever boy and did well – so well that his classmates revolted when the shepherd boy came out as top of the class. They carried him off and dug a hole in the desert, shoved him into it head first, and ran off. That's when he decided he had to be "the best."

Mohed later described his early life as a "disaster – tough, difficult, and painful," and his younger self as being "like an animal, driven towards the light." But, as he says, "all of us can change our destiny, can improve the world."

Given the chance for an education, studies became Mohed's mainstay. The top student in his class, he was sent to high school in Raqqa, the closest large Syrian town. Once again, he worked hard, copying from books he was unable to buy and spending hours in the library. At the age of 17 he was awarded the baccalaureate and a bursary to study petro-chemistry in France.

Arriving in Montpellier in Southern France, Mohed couldn't speak a word of French and didn't know anyone. Money was tight and he survived on one meal a day, but he devoted himself to studying and developed a passion for the French culture and language. He completed his education in Paris with a doctorate in information technology.

Years later he was to develop one of the world's first portable computers – weighing 20 kg.

Using the proceeds from the sale of his computer company, Mohed bought an insolvent scaffolding manufacturer in 1985 – the foundation for what would become the Altrad Group.

Transactions and alliances and a focus on **operations** have played an essential role in accelerating the growth of the Altrad Group. Mohed focused initially on buying distressed businesses. Being skilled at assessing value, he could swiftly identify and rectify loss-making operations by centralizing key functions such as recruitment, treasury management, and investment decisions. He now takes a longer-term approach, focusing on buying healthy, profitable businesses to grow market share and extending his range of products and services. In this way, he has created a network of more than 100 profitable subsidiaries, employing 39,000 staff in 100 countries.

A significant driver of his success – and his companies' staggering growth – is his ability to integrate and maximize the value of his acquisitions, coupled with his profound belief that the **customer** is king.

This success could not have been achieved without Mohed's personal values and management style, founded on an appreciation of the individual and a respect for cultural differences. The Altrad approach to **people, behaviors, and culture** is to place the individual at the center of the business. Mohed has long advocated for multiculturalism and respect for diversity.

Mohed said, "A business is first and foremost made by and for the men and women." Concern for his staff impacts company policy daily because "richness is individual and organized by the collective." He has an aversion to hierarchy and, when he buys a business, his aim is to impose a minimum of rules and leave most of the workforce and culture intact.

He has firm views on the role of business in society as well. "Don't look at a company just as a place that generates money," he says. "This is not the objective of life. The objective of life is to help humanity through action and effort."

With the recent acquisition of the Hertel, Prezioso, and Cape groups of companies, Mohed's sales are now US$4 billion,[1] making him one of the largest scaffold and building suppliers in the world, with a personal fortune of US$4 billion.[2]

Mohed's energy, resilience, and values have been, not surprisingly, drawn from his challenging childhood. As he sees it, you have to pay for your success with energy and time. He doesn't seem to need much sleep, working or writing up to 17 hours a day.

That determination to succeed, and his love for Montpellier, saw Mohed purchase the city's bankrupt rugby club in 2011. Thanks to his belief in himself and in his dreams, Montpellier's team is now playing in the first division of European rugby.

Today, due to the size of the Altrad Group, Mohed doesn't make all the decisions himself, but he keeps an eye on everything. "The due diligence and expertise now often come from people who are European and may not necessarily have the same culture as I do, so sometimes I need to intervene."

In addition to being named the EY World Entrepreneur Of The Year 2015, in 2005 the French government awarded Mohed the Legion of Honour (the equivalent of a knighthood) and, in 2015, Mohed joined the Forbes Billionaire List.

*   *   *

---

[1] "The Altrad Group Full-Year Results for 12 Month Period Ended August 2017," *Business Wire*, December 19, 2017.
[2] Mohed Altrad, https://www.forbes.com/profile/mohed-altrad/#c51a9265057e.

One of his greatest joys is literature and he has written four novels. The first, *Badawi* (meaning "Bedouin" in Arabic), combines autobiography and fiction, and records the difficult path taken by a child who runs away from his Syrian village, his family, and his country to escape his destiny as a shepherd. The work is built around the themes of desertion, uprooting, and the determination to succeed.

Mohed is a father to five children. "Writing, my business, and my family each have an equal place in my life. I have no wish to compromise any of these passions." He says he has waited his whole life to give the world this message: "We can all change our destiny and improve the world."

ILKKA PAANANEN
SUPERCELL
EY ENTREPRENEUR OF THE
YEAR 2015
FINLAND

Ilkka cofounded the global, multibillion dollar gaming company Supercell and has grown it with some unique perspectives on both talent and team structure and his innovative approaches to generating revenue. It has produced such blockbuster games as Clash of Clans and Hay Day.

Ilkka began his adult life with officer training in the coastal Finnish military – a good lesson in leadership, as he told Stephen Armstrong from *Wired* UK in 2018. "When you're leading people who aren't getting paid and you want them to follow you into battles, you learn a lot about motivation."

The son of two teachers, he was 22 when he, together with his friends, cofounded their first company: the digital games studio Sumea, which he sold to U.S. game maker Digital Chocolate in 2004. He remained with the newly merged company as president, running its European operations and overseeing its growth from 40 to 400 employees.

In 2010 Ilkka and his cofounders incorporated their new business, Supercell, based on his belief that people at all levels of the business would flourish if given the freedom, independence, and responsibility to be entrepreneurs.

Establishing a company with an ethos that ran counter to conventional thinking in gaming was not simple. Ilkka and his cofounders had to invest a significant amount of their personal savings to start the company. Also, during its first two years, Supercell struggled to produce any hit games.

In late 2011, they took the bold step of abandoning every project the company was working on and bet everything on a mobile tablet-only strategy. This meant "killing" games with hundreds of thousands of users on Facebook and dedicating every resource to new projects. The strategy worked well.

Turnover grew from US$226,000 to more than $2 billion in just five years. In 2015 Supercell made US$924 million profit on revenues of $2.3 billion. Every member of his staff is a shareholder and has benefitted from this result.[3]

An essential part of Ilkka's growth has been his intense focus on **people, behaviors, and culture**. Supercell was founded on the idea that the company's management should focus on finding the best people, create a culture that enabled them to do what they do best, and then get out of the way – so they can get on with it. This is encapsulated in the phrase "the best teams make the best games." So convinced is he of this that in the same 2018 *Wired* interview he said, "When you're recruiting, make sure you personally interview everyone you hire – no exceptions."

This is so fundamental to Supercell that it's reflected in the name. The company is made up of independent "cells," small

[3] "With Just 3 Games, Supercell Made $924M in Profits on $2.3B in Revenue in 2015," Venturebeat.com, March 9, 2016.

teams of highly talented people who are given complete responsibility for what they do – almost like a start-up within a start-up.

The ultimate benchmark is Ilkka's self-characterization as "the worlds least powerful CEO." The fewer decisions he must make, the more his teams are fulfilling his vision of quality through independence and responsibility.

In an interview in 2013, Ilkka identified key behaviors for getting the most from his staff:

- Be transparent. "We send a daily email with all key performance indicators to everyone in the company."
- Celebrate failure. "You must eliminate the fear of failure. You need to take risks to succeed and for that you must take away the fear from that risk."

Ilkka attributes much of his success to "choosing employees like a sports team" – get the best players, create the best environment for them, and let them get on with it.

"The best sports teams get a lot of strong and talented personalities to play together really well," he says. "It is super competitive, like the start-up world, and the element of luck is key to both. I used to think the winning team was the one with well thought-out plans and everything beautifully organized, and split into boxes and timelines and budgets, but that's not how creativity works."

In an industry that often imposes commercial deadlines and top-down mandates on its creative staff, this is innovative stuff. At Supercell, teams are given the freedom to work on their own game ideas and to set their own timetables. Perhaps most important, teams make their own decisions as to whether what they have produced hits the company's bar for quality. The individual team working on each game, not management, makes those decisions.

"The biggest thing I learned through my career is that building a business is all about the team and the people," Ilkka says. "In the end, nothing else matters."

The second area which Ilkka attributes to driving growth is understanding what the **customer** appreciates and creating a business model and products that meet those customer needs and preferences. Quality is at the center of his product strategy: Products that are popular for a period of time but have a short shelf life have largely defined the mobile game industry. Companies attempt to move from hit to hit in a matter of months, and churn out a large number of games to increase the chances of that happening. Supercell has turned this strategy on its head, focusing instead on games as services that will maintain and deepen the interest and engagement of players over the years.

The risk paid off with the launch of the company's first two mobile games in mid-2012, Clash of Clans and Hay Day, which both went quickly to the top of the charts for Apple's iPhone/iPad platform and have remained there ever since.

In an industry where most companies release several titles in the hope that one or two will succeed, releasing only those you believe will be long-term successes is a risky strategy. Ilkka has staked the company on it.

Supercell has also pioneered the "free-to-play" model in mobile gaming. Here, users download games for free and are later given the option of purchasing "in-game" items for real money. Unlike many other titles, all the content in all of Supercell's games is available free to users. Players have total control of their experience and can play a full Supercell game without being forced to pay.

Ilkka Paananen, cofounder and CEO of Helsinki-based mobile games developer Supercell, is just 40. But he and Supercell – by revenue, the world's biggest video games company – are among Finland's highest taxpayers.[4]

---

[4] "Supercell Brought Almost €1bn in Tax Revenue to Finland in 2016," *Helsinki Times*, November 2, 2017; "Pocket Gamer.Biz Top 50 Developer 2017," pocketgamer.biz, https://www.pocketgamer.biz/list/66597/top-50-mobile-game-developers-of-2017/.

Across the globe, more than 100 million people each day play Supercell's free titles: Clash of Clans, Boom Beach, Hay Day, and Clash Royale.

Set up in 2010, Supercell now has a market capitalization of US$10 billion. In 2016 alone, in-game purchases of his products generated US$2.3 billion in revenue, making it a modern money tree.

In 2017, Supercell announced that it earned a profit of US$810 million on revenues of $2.029 billion – an enviable financial accomplishment for a company that didn't release a game globally in 2017, and has only released four games in its seven-year life.[5]

Recognized for his ability to scale companies from founding to successful commercial operations, Ilkka is sought out for a number of activities outside his own entrepreneurial exploits, including his involvement as a Partner, Advisor, or Entrepreneur-in-Residence with Lifeline Ventures, Atomico, and others and has been a coach for the venture accelerator program at Aalto Venture Garage. In addition to being selected as the EY Entrepreneur Of The Year 2015 Finland, Ilkka served as a member of the independent judging panel for the EY World Entrepreneur Of The Year awards.

*   *   *

Ilkka and his team place a lot of importance on sharing the benefits of their financial success. Ilkka, together with his cofounder Mikko Kodisoja, founded We-Foundation, a philanthropic trust that focuses on helping marginalized kids, youth, and their families, donating €200 million to launch the foundation. In addition, Ilkka and his cofounders have also invested millions of dollars into Finnish start-ups, as part of his dream to make Helsinki the Silicon Valley of Europe.

---

[5] "Supercell 2017 Results: $810 Million in Profit and $2 Billion in Revenue – Without a New Game," Venturebeat.com, February 14, 2018.

DAME ROSEMARY SQUIRE
DIRECTOR
TRAFALGAR
ENTERTAINMENT GROUP
CO-FOUNDER
AMBASSADOR THEATRE
GROUP
EY ENTREPRENEUR OF THE
YEAR 2014
UNITED KINGDOM

London is renowned throughout the world for its live theater experiences and Dame Rosemary Squire is one of the most innovative, well-known, and highly respected players in the business for her knowledge of all aspects of successful theater funding and operations and her many customer experience innovations.

Unlike many women of her generation, Rosemary's mother had the benefit of a university education and was determined that her daughters would follow suit. Rosemary, the youngest child in a family of girls, was brought up knowing it was "good to be bright and to study."

She gained a BA with first class honors in modern languages from Southampton University, studied at the University in Barcelona, and completed postgraduate study at Ivy League

Brown University in the United States. "My family saw education as I do, as a tool," she says.

That tool was first put to work when 16-year-old Rosemary sat on the steps of the Playhouse Theatre Nottingham and thought, "This is what I want to do. I love the stories and I love the worlds that are created here." She knew her strengths were not in acting but in theater management. Even then, she says, "I understood a bit about money and about how deals were put together." She was always self-confident and thinks her ability with languages helped her "absorb things."

Along the way, she struck obstacles. In her twenties, her first child was born with Down syndrome and she was made redundant from a senior position while on maternity leave with her second. These experiences shaped her attitude toward hard work and drew her toward a career as an entrepreneur, where she could work for herself, on her own terms, and with the freedom to realize her full potential.

True to her motto, "You must be the change you want to see in the world," Rosemary pioneered a ground-breaking business **operations** model that successfully combines three large aspects of theater – production, theater operation, and ticketing – into one company. She has done almost every job in theater, working her way up from tearing tickets via the box office, to producing and financial management, to the boardroom – where, as CEO, she led acquisitions, integration, and investor relations.

Rosemary was also willing to take risks: She mortgaged her home and sold her car to finance her businesses during a time of economic uncertainty. Her first regional theater opened during a recession and her largest acquisition was made during the 2009 financial crisis. But despite adverse economic conditions, the companies maintained strong growth and twice delivered significant profit to shareholders when they were sold.

With her first company, the Ambassador Theatre Group (ATG), Rosemary needed to raise **funding and finance** to buy her first theaters. This meant persuading investors that theater was a legitimate business prospect, with significant potential. At first, she tapped into a group of like-minded people with money to invest, before moving to corporate investors to acquire seven West End houses in 2000.

After paying £30 million for these venues, she had only nine months to prove herself to her investors. This experience proved crucial when, in 2009, the company sought private equity financing for its largest acquisition. Again, showing her appetite for risk and her self-belief, Rosemary remortgaged her family home to invest more money into her business.

Rosemary grew the organization she cofounded from a small family business into a global success story through her imagination, drive, and enthusiasm for new ways of working. Examples of this innovation include revenue management, the first organization in the United Kingdom to use a cross-departmental team, working with a range of partners from venues to visiting producers, and maximizing income and driving occupancy through reporting and analysis, dynamic pricing, competitive fee structures, and loyalty schemes.

These initiatives also include the Ambassador lounges – premium bars aimed at increasing the time customers spend in theaters – and Ordertorium – the first at-seat service at any theater, allowing drinks and food orders to be taken, paid for, and delivered in the auditorium using app technology.

The company Rosemary founded today employs more than 4,000 people and owns more than 50 live theaters globally. She attributes her success in part to her commitment to developing **people, behaviors, and culture** – hiring managers and senior colleagues whose skills complement hers – people who want to grow and embrace change, and to seize opportunities alongside her.

After selling the ATG group of companies in 2013, Rosemary and her husband, Howard Panter, have now come full circle. Stepping down from ATG in 2016, they are now working with a group of family and friends to do it all over again with their new company, the Trafalgar Entertainment Group.

"There Is Nothing Like a Dame" – nothing in the world! The *South Pacific* song title has special relevance to the 30-year theater career of Dame Rosemary Squire. At Windsor Castle in February 2018, Rosemary was made a Dame Commander of the Order of the British Empire for her services to theater and philanthropy.

Sitting in the front row was her 91-year-old mother, who was "tickled pink" to see her youngest daughter honored by the sovereign. Also at her side was husband and fellow theater entrepreneur, Sir Howard Panter, who had been knighted four years earlier.

Being clear about her destination has allowed Rosemary to make the journey from selling tickets in a box office to being named, with Sir Howard, as the most influential people in British theater for seven consecutive years – and to Rosemary being named the most prominent woman in theater during the modern era by *The Stage* 100 list.

In addition to these honors, Rosemary became the first woman to be named the EY Entrepreneur Of The Year 2014 in the United Kingdom and represent her country in Monte Carlo at the EY World Entrepreneur Of The Year competition. In 2017, she served as an EY World Entrepreneur Of The Year judge.

* * *

Rosemary's experiences underpin her public advocacy for equal opportunity for women in the workplace and she has become an international role model for women who want to run their own businesses.

Rosemary has taken what she's learned from her business success and passion for education and given back to the United Kingdom in many ways: She has raised almost £10 million to establish the Squire Performing Arts Centre for her alma mater; chairs the Great Ormond Street Hospitals Tick Tock Appeal, raising over £18 m to date; sat on the National Arts Council for nine years; and chairs the Southwest Art Council.

*   *   *

As the vignettes on the previous pages suggest, being a successful entrepreneur means continually "daring to compete" – going through transformative times in both personal and business lives. For some, it is a decision to leave the relative comfort of a successful career to pursue the dream of controlling one's own destiny. For all, it is a series of bold decisions taken to drive their personal growth and that of their company:

- Innovative new business models and incorporating new technologies
- Important strategic partnerships or acquisitions
- Developing new products or services that meet the changing demands of customers
- Executing game-changing financial transactions including public offerings
- Entering new markets
- Continually building teams of talented people and the culture and values that will sustain growth
- Identifying and managing risks

Now that you have met them, you understand their incredible stories – how they overcame personal hardships and seized business opportunities to build truly market-leading, world-class companies. We are confident that the "collective wisdom" they have shared will further enhance the relevance of our EY 7 Drivers of Growth framework, as explained in more detail in the next chapters.

Understanding EY's 7 Drivers of Growth

EY has over 30 years' experience supporting entrepreneurs from start-up to market leaders. In order to consolidate our knowledge from that experience to be able to provide better insights to entrepreneurs, we researched 250 EY Entrepreneur Of The Year winners and worked with 500 EY member-firm partners to access lessons from several thousand businesses. Based on this research we created the EY 7 Drivers of Growth – our unique insight into how to accelerate growth (see Figure P3.1).

FIGURE P3.1 The EY 7 Drivers of Growth

Our research identified three stages of maturity through which entrepreneurial companies progress:

1. Developing
2. Established
3. Leading

At each stage of maturity, we mapped leading practices from the best businesses globally in all industries. These are outlined in the first figure at the beginning of the next seven chapters.

Not surprisingly, we found that Customer was the most significant Growth Driver. Leaders of a successful business put the customer at the center of everything they do. Traditional thinking suggests that customer value is generated by focus on people, systems, and processes. Our research confirmed this, although we open up the descriptions of these relationships:

- People, behavior, and culture
- Digital technology and analytics
- Operations

Today we find an extraordinary pace of change in two of the drivers that are affecting company leaders across the world. In People we observe a new generation entering the workforce with very different expectations. New, younger CEOs are driving fresh ways of thinking and working in the market place. They are building flatter organizations, with empowered teams working in less siloed disciplines.

In Digital we see a number of transformations including the increasing power and value of data, the rapid advance of artificial intelligence, robotic process automation, blockchain, and all the change that emanates from new cognitive technologies.

We also identify additional Drivers of Growth that we discuss in later chapters:

- Transactions and alliances
- Funding and finance
- Risk

Not all successful enterprises have achieved Leading maturity in all seven drivers; in fact, we have yet to find a company that matches that profile. Every business leader plots his or her growth journey. Every leadership team has ambition to deliver more than their capability allows in any period, and makes choices about their priorities.

However, we find that businesses that manage a balance across all seven drivers do grow the fastest. For example, businesses thinking of expanding internationally would act to ensure that their product or service was right for the new market (customer); they would consider whether to fund centrally or locally, and understand local taxes and regulations, capital ownership rules, and how to repatriate profits (funding and finance). They would research local employment laws and also get the right mix of local and central human resources to maintain corporate values and brand while securing acceptance from local communities (people, behavior, and culture).

From our many interactions across the world, we mapped key activities that we saw the very best doing for each of the drivers on their journey to market leadership. We identified three key stages of maturity in each driver from developing to market leading.

In the coming chapters, we discuss each of the drivers in detail. We explore the particular experiences of the Entrepreneurs. As you read, we encourage you to learn from their experiences and to reflect on your own business.

Driver #1: Customer

"No customers, no business"

From the outset, leading companies make customers their focal point (see Figure 7.1). They understand that by putting customers' needs and desires first, they can achieve a competitive advantage. They know all about their customers – who they are, what they want, and when they want it – and they know that building customer loyalty goes hand in hand with long-term sustainable growth. Even after becoming market leaders, these companies are constantly thinking about how to keep delivering for each and every customer in all markets in which they operate. They don't stand still.

Leading
The business is focused on providing a differentiated customer experience by predicting customers' needs and delivering personalized value.

Established
The business is focused on customer satisfaction. Customer engagement is information-led.

Developing
The business is focused on product and service. There is a strong emphasis on sales growth.

FIGURE 7.1 EY 7 Drivers of Growth – Customer

Having a strong customer focus in turn means having a strong offering in each of these areas:

- Customer experience
- Products, markets, and channels
- Marketing
- Sales and pricing

"The best entrepreneurs understand that their customers must be at the center of everything they do," says Edwina Fitzmaurice, EY Global Advisory Markets, Business Development, Sector and Solutions Leader. "Whether leveraging digital technologies to enhance the customer experience, improving operations and supply chain to ensure efficient and effective delivery of goods and services demanded by customers, or using data analytics to truly understand customer behaviors, successful entrepreneurs use many levers to rapidly grow their companies."

The Entrepreneurs are intensely focused on their customers. They provide a repeatable customer experience and ensure that it meets and exceeds their customers' expectations, including the digital experience. They develop innovative products and services, frictionless sales and distribution channels, and competitive sales and pricing models.

"The customer is number one. If you don't have a customer, you don't have a business," says Craig Heatley, founder, Rainbow Corporation and SKY TV. "The first focus must be the customer. There are great examples of big companies that haven't done that. Either they haven't focused on the customer or they haven't been aware of a change in the environment – the two go hand in hand. I have never consciously thought about the customers; it is like breathing – without that you have nothing else, so it is just so fundamental. I have never thought I needed to tell my people about the customer, because the customer is where any business will start and finish."

Leading companies focus on continually improving all aspects of the customer experience. They understand that achieving and sustaining high levels of customer satisfaction drives revenue growth and often leads to long-term competitive advantage in the marketplace. Leaders in this space proactively listen and solicit feedback from their customers to improve products, services, and the overall customer experience. Increasingly this listening and soliciting derives not only through personal interaction but also from data analytics that identify customer behaviors and predicts trends.

"We have tried to be innovative to improve the customer experience," explains Dame Rosemary Squire of Trafalgar Entertainment Group.

"Put your customers' needs first and understand what they really need rather than what they think they want and you will be successful," adds Olivia Lum of Hyflux Ltd.

The Entrepreneurs are obsessive about building and maintaining long-term relationships with their customers. They are in constant dialogue with them and put them at the center of everything they do. What converts this into real value is their ability to listen and understand their customer needs and embed this into the culture of their businesses.

"I like to talk to people," says Jim Nixon of Nixon Energy Investments. "They say to me that it is so nice of me to come and talk to them and I tell them that it is my pleasure. I ask, What could I do to improve? How can we help you do a better job to serve our customers?"

"Customer delight is what we focus on day in and day out. In this digital world, I think the customer span is also short as a customer can like or dislike you in a matter of seconds," says Uday Kotak of Kotak Mahindra Bank.

Digital technology and social media have made it exceptionally easy for customers to take their business elsewhere. Comparison sites can highlight pricing differentials in seconds; a poor experience can be communicated on social media platforms to thousands of people globally.

"The customer's only loyalty is to their last visit," says Michael Wu of Maxim Group. "If they had a great visit, they will tell their friends. If they had a bad experience at any one of our restaurants, the first time they may forgive us, but the second time they won't come back. There is no such thing as loyalty for loyalty's sake. The only loyalty you can create is by giving them a reason to come back."

Products, markets, and channels

At the most basic level, entrepreneurs satisfy the needs of their customers by selling products and services through various markets and channels. Increasingly, customers expect greater choice – not only in the range of products and services that they can purchase, but also in the digital and bricks-and-mortar channels through which they can access them. Again, data analytics can provide real insight into customer preferences that the best entrepreneurs monitor and to which they quickly respond.

These markets and channels typically include geographic as well as specific functional groups and market segments. Companies need to monitor their specific products, markets, and channels for new opportunities as well as assess current sales results against goals (e.g., by product line, SKU, geography), and introduce corrective action strategies should sales trends begin to flatten. These strategies may include new marketing and pricing models or may suggest that innovation of the products and services is required in order to stay relevant and competitive.

The Entrepreneurs understand that market and consumer preferences are constantly changing. By keeping close to them, by continually probing to understand the needs of the customer (and end-consumer, when different), and by innovating all aspects of the supply chain, they are able to keep ahead of the competition, frequently creating new markets. Their agility means they are able to respond more quickly than competitors to deliver innovative and successful products and services to the market in a very short timescale.

The Entrepreneurs we interviewed expanded their businesses internationally very early in their growth cycle in order to continue to grow. This was driven by customer needs and also the need to protect their businesses from individual country downturns.

"We must understand the customer's needs and do things backwards," says Olivia Lum of Hyflux Ltd. "We don't develop something and push it to market and force the customer to adopt what we have developed. You must understand the customer first. You don't spend your time within four walls and dream about something the customer does not want; you go out there, you talk to more people, you observe. I tell my market development people, 'observe, listen, and see exactly what the customer desires.'"

Our Entrepreneurs hire people with diverse skills to build empathy with the customer that is reflected in product design and in the markets that they expand into. They are serial disruptors – always looking for a way to bring new thinking to existing products or to open up in new markets. They have an insatiable appetite for growth.

"We are all consciously looking for gaps in the market that we can disrupt and deliver products that will stop kids in their tracks," says Manny Stul of Moose Toys. "If an opportunity doesn't fit that criteria then we don't do it. We are fastidious about 'being different' and we challenge our teams to set the trends, not follow them.

"We have most likely bypassed good product opportunities, but I can genuinely state that what makes our jobs fulfilling is the challenge to create something different, knowing that we are helping redefine how kids play with toys, especially in the collectible channel."

Some entrepreneurs have soared to success by finding an untapped, unloved market. Rubens Menin of MRV Engenharia is one such. "I have always evaluated the 'low income' market as the one with the highest potential in Brazil, logically looking at demographics in relation to income. I was also interested in the scale and opportunity for industrialization that is a characteristic of the segment."

Marketing

"Companies are the brand owners but customers are the owners of the brand's reputation," says José Rosenberg, Colchones Rosen SAIC and EY Entrepreneur Of The Year 2018 Chile.

Marketing involves making it easy and essential for customers to buy from you. Over the years, traditional marketing has focused on the four Ps: product, price, placement, and promotion. Yet today's marketing mix also requires additional focus on the overall brand strategy, specific market/cultural packaging changes, websites, Apps, social media, and other digital elements necessary to successfully compete in today's global business environment.

Increasingly, the most successful brands today – many of them created by high-growth entrepreneurs – have a very clear brand identity that includes not only product or service attributes but also clear positioning on social responsibility and purpose.

The Entrepreneurs leverage their ability to build long-term relationships with customers and to build innovative products and services that create markets. Their marketing capitalizes on these strengths to build a brand that is a true differentiator. Their customers are frequently brand ambassadors for them, giving them competitive advantage that drives increased sales and margin.

Entrepreneurs have always been very quick to identify and exploit creative approaches to marketing. More recently, they have developed innovative and responsive digital marketing, integrated with traditional methods, while harnessing the value of social media.

"We were the first people to make webisodes," says Manny Stul of Moose Toys. "Very soon one of the American companies that copied Shopkins (children's toys) came up with a variation and we found out that they had contacted our Australian webisode people to replicate what we were doing. Yes, we are the leaders and the pioneers but it's not unusual for a good innovative product to be copied – we just must keep innovating and we have to do things differently and work harder."

Sales and Pricing

Sales are the lifeblood of any enterprise – companies need to identify, secure, and sustain customer relationships to stay in business. In addition to defining and managing the sales process, companies need to price their products and services effectively to generate their desired margins. Making the sale, however, is only the first step in the process of nurturing long-term customer relationships.

Sustainable customer relationships, together with strong brands and reputations, are a significant driver of sales. The Entrepreneurs harness the power of their customer data. They have become expert at collecting, storing, and analyzing it to drive detailed customer segmentation and, ultimately, efficient and effective targeted sales and marketing activity.

One thing is certain in today's market – change is the norm. We live with changes in demographics, buying behavior, and the globalization of markets. Entrepreneurs thrive in this environment and are typically ahead of the game, anticipating rather than responding to change.

"Data and analytics are so important in our business. An example is that live theater has been slow: the adoption curve of dynamic pricing for airlines and pop concerts has been well ahead of that for live theater, says Dame Rosemary Squire of Trafalgar Entertainment Group. "Looking at demand and making sure that the economics work is imperative. You need to keep very tight controls over the economics of producing a production because each production is a mini joint venture with other partners. You capitalize it in the same way you would a company. You drive the revenues by looking at what's selling and which performances and moving the ticket price accordingly."

Pricing is as much an art as it is a mathematical calculation. Arriving at the right price isn't as simple as undercutting the competition. "If you and I decided to start a new drink brand to compete with a global brand …," suggests Craig Heatley, founder, Rainbow Corporation and SKY TV. "We have done our research and the global brand sells for a dollar a can, and we are going to sell for 50 cents. Don't think that the global brand won't reduce their price to 50 cents. That competitive response is something that people don't usually factor into their business plans."

And pricing doesn't exist in a vacuum: it is intrinsically part of the whole product or brand experience and impacts on every stakeholder in the enterprise. "We see our business as a three-legged stool," explains Linda Hasenfratz of Linamar Corporation. "If a customer wants a big price decrease I say we would love to do that for you but I have employees, I have shareholders. ... It's a very simple and powerful illustration, a three-legged stool, and of course keeping it in balance so you don't tip over is very easy to visualize, which is always going to be the most effective way to portray something."

While our exceptional Entrepreneurs monitor the competition, they do not adhere blindly to market pricing. They understand that discounting prices is rarely an effective strategy to achieving sustainable market leadership. "In the late 1980s, when the bank was entering the car finance business, Citibank was the market leader," says Uday Kotak of Kotak Mahindra Bank. "But lenders had one big constraint – cars were in short supply, meaning even the market leader could finance only a limited number of vehicles. So we decided to buy cars in advance and sell them only to customers who were buying their finance through our bank. We charged no premium on the car sales and the strategy proved hugely successful."

In Uday Kotak's case, entering a new market was about understanding the whole supply chain. Sometimes it is about speed and efficiency. "If a company wants to be competitive in the market, innovation must always be a priority and happen in a continuous mode," says Rubens Menin, of MRV Engenharia. "Our construction process today, the result of significant investment in research both in Brazil and abroad, allows the company to build on high-speed time."

The last word on Customer belongs to the late Steve Jobs, founder of Apple Inc., who cautions against giving the customer what he or she wants. "People don't know what they want until you show it to them," he says. "That's why I never rely on market research. Our job is to read things that are not yet on the page."[1]

---

[1] *BusinessWeek* (May 25, 1998).

8

Driver #2: People, Behaviors, and Culture

"Cutting stone or building a cathedral?"

Any organization is only ever as good as the people working for it. To win the war for talent, leading entrepreneurs build an environment that values diversity and attracts and retains the right people to help grow their businesses – not just great people, but people who share the company's vision and fit its culture (see Figure 8.1). Leading businesses provide strong leadership and create an inclusive environment where differences are valued and people can innovate to drive the business forward. On top of this they invest in their employees, nurturing their talents and helping them develop skills to match the changing demands of the business during each different growth phase.

Leading
High performance is expected, responsibilities are delegated, and the People Plan is fundamental to strategy.

Established
There is the flexibility and capability to meet the needs of an evolving business. Management is increasingly focused on the future, people, succession, and sustainability.

Developing
Management exhibits entrepreneurial spirit. Managers are hands-on and lead by example.

FIGURE 8.1 EY 7 Drivers of Growth – People, behaviors, and culture

"We need people who are able to think in terms of business processes and translate them into digital language," says Natalie Mekelburger, EY Entrepreneur Of The Year 2017 Germany and CEO of automotive parts manufacturer Coroplast. "To attract such talent, we create a stimulating and secure work environment. We also develop our employee brand by staying true to our company values and being top of the market in engineering quality and customer service."

Our research shows that entrepreneurial success in the area of people, behaviors, and culture comes from four key areas:

1. Capability – they recruit, train, and retain talent to ensure that they have the right skills at the right time.
2. Leadership – they attract and develop leaders who collectively understand the purpose of the business and create and enforce a set of values that drive sustainable growth.
3. Performance management and rewards – they are able to motivate and inspire their people to get the most out of them and derive optimal performance from the business. They reward behavior as well as performance through a blend of short- and long-term incentives.
4. Innovation – they create an environment that encourages and rewards innovation at all levels of the business, and ensures that failure is seen as a learning opportunity.

Capability

In the war for talent, all businesses face the challenge of attracting, training, and retaining the best people to meet the needs of the business. This challenge is particularly relevant to entrepreneurs whose needs change as their business moves through different phases, from start-up to market leader.

In the early days, entrepreneurs need to attract a combination of young innovative individuals and more experienced leaders. The current generation of young people entering the workplace has many different expectations than did previous generations. On the one hand, they are prepared to take risks and are less likely than previous generations to build their careers with one employer. On the other hand, they have very high expectations and increasingly demand a work-life balance that previous generations failed to achieve. In response to this, entrepreneurs provide a very different working environment to many major corporations. Differences may include more relaxed working spaces and dress codes, flatter organizational structures with less vertiginous hierarchies, more flexible working arrangements facilitated by new technology, and rewards that are more closely linked to success of the business. These collaborative and flexible characteristics make the prospect of working for entrepreneurial companies very attractive.

"I think the old days of 90-hour weeks are gone and people need to find a balance in their lives," agrees Jim Nixon of Nixon Energy Investments. "I think that we can achieve that balance without losing efficiency because of the capability and technology that is now available."

Attracting experienced leaders into early-stage entrepreneurial companies is far more challenging. With experience and age come responsibilities such as dependent children, a mortgage, and other financial commitments that make the risk of working for a young company difficult. However, experienced people are often attracted to an exciting corporate story, a visionary leader, the opportunity to make a meaningful impact, and equity participation that may have a significant upside.

"Apart from the initial four or five people who came with me, it was very difficult to hire people because the company's early reputation was very poor," says Nixon. "But as soon as we started winning a couple of big contracts, people started taking notice and within a few years people were coming to our door for jobs. A lot of it was word of mouth. If you get good people, they invariably know good people. If you are building a platform for success, then people are attracted to it."

Of course, however stringent your recruitment criteria, you will occasionally make a mistake. "Managing people out of the business is very tricky; you must sift out the ones that are passengers," says Dame Rosemary Squire of Trafalgar Entertainment Group. "You must be rigorous and have proper review mechanisms, proper goals, proper targets that people must achieve."

The Entrepreneurs tend to have a strong belief that getting a person with the right attitude is more important than skills. With this approach, experience is always subordinate to character. As the great management thinker Tom Peters says, "Hire for attitude and train for skills."

Core to both attracting and retaining great talent is the creation of a great entrepreneurial environment. More important than the physical environment is the culture of your company. Talent will be attracted by an inspirational leader with a highly motivated team around him or her, a strong sense of purpose, a nurturing team culture that operates a bit like a family, and a vibrant can-do culture.

"Two stone cutters meet and the first one asks, 'what are you doing?' The second one replies, 'I'm just cutting stone.' And the first guy says, 'I am on a team that's building a cathedral.' That's the difference," says Craig Heatley of Rainbow Corporation and SKY TV.

To harness your team in the service of a big idea – a cathedral – is a winning formula. As writer and speaker Simon Sinek says, "People don't buy *what* you do, they buy *why* you do it."

For a team to work well, it needs to be diverse. A team of identical superstars will always be outperformed by a mixed group of people with different skills and approaches.

"We attribute much of our success to choosing our employees like a sports team," says Ilkka Paananen of Supercell. "We believe that teams with diversity have a greater chance of achieving great results; different points of view enrich each other and result in a better outcome. Also, as we create games for the global market it makes sense that the more global the team behind the game, the greater the chance of success for the game."

Entrepreneurs focused on attracting great people to accelerate their growth embrace this diversity and know how to harness it. "I want gender diversity, cultural diversity, I want diversity of thought and opinion," says Murad Al-Katib of AGT Food and Ingredients Inc. "I think great leaders surround themselves with people that are absolutely the opposite of themselves – and that they feel empowered by the diversity and not threatened by it."

Once a company has grown from the initial start-up phase, the challenge is to keep that excitement and entrepreneurial spirit alive. The talented team that had such autonomy as you built your business from the ground up is now involved in managing processes and bureaucracy. One way of giving individuals new challenges as well as an understanding of different areas of the business is job rotation.

"We give all our senior management the opportunity to rotate jobs," says Uday Kotak of Kotak Mahindra Bank. "When you throw people out of their comfort zone, it gives very good output."

Leadership

The vision, drive, and passion of our elite group of winning Entrepreneurs have an enormous impact on attracting and retaining the best people. Their ability to constantly connect with and motivate people is very powerful and they manage to maintain this even as their businesses grow bigger and more complex. They ensure that the purpose, values, and culture of the business are understood by all and infused throughout the business. They "walk the talk," not relying on layers of management to communicate the culture, but directly interacting with staff at all levels.

"I have always been a big believer in the importance of going into the plant and spending time with people physically, not on the phone, not by email," says Linda Hasenfratz of Linamar Group. "It is the best way to ensure a culture is well understood. By asking questions when you walk around, the comments and observations that you make by sitting with the people, that's what they remember. It's fine to put together a strategy and say, okay, these are the things we are going to focus on this year, but if you never ask anybody a question about how they are implementing the strategy then you know that's clearly not how you want the business run."

This ability to lead from the top to the bottom marks out exceptional leaders. "A good leader builds management teams that recognize talent; they communicate their vision," says Murad Al-Katib of AGT Food and Ingredients Inc. "A great leader can do the same thing, but they have a different recognition; diversity and leadership is one of the most important things to go from being good to great."

Performance management and rewards

The ability of entrepreneurs to share their vision, drive, and passion with their teams leads to another important outcome – it encourages people at all levels to think and behave as if they own the business.

"A culture of accountability is very important to success in any business," says Linda Hasenfratz of Linamar Group. "We like the idea of people doing their jobs and acting like they have ownership and making decisions as if they are the owner."

The Entrepreneurs, focused on growth, develop and deploy a mix of short-term and long-term performance targets that include a focus on behaviors as well as outcomes. Cultural fit is often a primary selection criterion during recruitment and the importance of understanding and living the values of the company is reflected in both performance measures and rewards.

Early stage businesses are generally very focused on short-term growth. Without it they die. Once established, however, the introduction of longer-term objectives and rewards is common. Achievement is rated and rewarded across individual, team, and business performance measures.

The introduction of an employee share ownership scheme is also common and often more effective than equivalent corporate employee equity programs. The business valuations of entrepreneurial companies tend to grow dramatically and employees share in that growth. This is particularly relevant when hiring for key leadership positions.

"I always work on three stages of incentives. I always incentivize the whole company. If the business is successful, every single person in that business will get a bonus at the end of the year," says Jim Nixon of Nixon Energy Investments.

Innovation

Entrepreneurs are natural innovators. It is fundamental to their success. Rarely can a company beat their competitors by copying what they do. To become a market leader you need to find ways to innovate and leapfrog your competition.

Companies generally pass through innovation cycles.

Early stage businesses focus on innovation in everything they do – everyone in the business feels very involved. It is a very exciting time, when successes are celebrated. It is a time of high growth and often very little profit. It is a time when the business is agile and can respond quickly to new ideas and initiatives.

However, as businesses become more established, they typically move into a phase of focusing on streamlining operations (discussed in detail in Chapter 10 ahead). During this period, formal roles are created, reporting structures are put in place, and a more functional leadership team is formed. As the business becomes more efficient and effective, profitable growth ensues.

The challenge with this evolution, though, is that the added structures can change the culture and impede agility. The downside risk is that some who were involved when the business was in its early stage – the innovators – start to feel detached from the business. They may be less involved with leadership decisions and are at risk of leaving or being hired away to newer companies. Furthermore, new layers of approval may cause business decisions to take longer to make and slow execution that may frustrate high flyers.

It is sometimes difficult, as the focus pivots to operational efficiency, to maintain that culture of innovation, and yet without it, no enterprise achieves or maintains market leadership. During the middle age of company evolution, it's vital to take specific steps to ensure innovation doesn't take a back seat. Some companies give individual leaders or teams specific responsibility for innovation, creating small experimental labs within the company to try out new products, services, or models. Others ensure that every staff member is tasked with thinking creatively, of risking failure. One of the hallmarks of market leaders is their ability to keep innovation alive during this transition phase from startup to multinational corporation.

"One of the things people struggle with as their business grows is how to go from an entrepreneurial culture to one of more controls," says Linda Hasenfratz of Linamar Group. "You want to maintain the entrepreneurial culture and you want to maintain the individuality of plants or groups in running their businesses and making their own decisions without creating undue risk. We like to talk to our people about a sort of a continuum of corporate control."

The Entrepreneurs are successful in large part due to their ability to find, develop, and retain the best talent to help them accelerate the growth of their ventures. They find ways of communicating their passion and purpose to all their staff and don't lose their natural impetus to innovate as the pressure to create processes and efficiencies grows with size.

9

Driver #3: Digital Technology and Analytics

"The new industrial revolution"

"It's no longer possible to think of the physical and digital as two separate worlds," says Angela Ahrendts, SVP Apple Retail, and before that, CEO of Burberry, in an interview with the *Financial Times*.[1] Digital technology is transforming how products are made, how they are sold, how we work, and the quantity and sophistication of a company's information bank. For entrepreneurial business leaders, that information is power. It can help make better, quicker, smarter decisions that improve business performance as well as manage risk (see Figure 9.1).

Leading
Digital is a primary driver of customer value and business strategy and this innovation has redefined the business model and the products and services offered.

Established
The business embraces digital channels, analytics, and other digital technologies to benefit the company and its customers.

Developing
Technology is leveraged in core functions. The business is more likely to adopt cloud.

FIGURE 9.1 EY 7 Drivers of Growth – Digital technology and analytics

[1] https://www.ft.com/content/7d55c2ca-bc77-11e2-9519-00144feab7de.

The World Economic Forum describes this transformation as the Fourth Industrial Revolution – one that will be at least as far-reaching as the industrial revolutions that preceded it. "The Fourth Industrial Revolution – the current period of rapid, simultaneous, and systemic transformation driven by advances in science and technology – is reshaping industries, blurring geographical boundaries, challenging existing regulatory frameworks, and even redefining what it means to be human."[2]

But some legacy businesses may find it harder to harness the full power that digital technology offers. While most business leaders recognize the potential value that going digital brings, some still find it hard to successfully leverage information technology to deliver business change. Not our elite winning Entrepreneurs, however. Each has used innate agility to respond quickly to the fast-moving pace of technological change and use it to competitive advantage.

EY's global Growth Barometer survey recently highlighted the significant pace of this change. In 2017, 74% of businesses said that they would *never* adopt artificial intelligence (AI). Twelve months later, 67% said they *would* be adopting AI within the next two years. This extraordinary shift of opinion is testament to the pace of change driven by new cognitive technologies.[3]

"We are already preparing for the digitally connected world of the future," says Natalie Mekelburger, EY Entrepreneur Of The Year 2017 Germany. "For sure, [artificial intelligence] will be at center stage in our production processes as well as product development."

At the EY World Entrepreneur Of The Year final in Monaco in June 2018, more than 500 entrepreneurs discussed changes to the business world and to jobs. These entrepreneurs

---

[2] *Source:* World Economic Forum.
[3] *Source:* 2018 EY Growth Barometer survey.

are at the forefront of driving technological change. They see both the threat and the opportunity. They understand that to compete in the new world they must answer two primary questions:

1. How do I lead from the front in adopting new technology in every aspect of my business?
2. How do I change my business model to create new skills and roles to drive and sustain this change in technology – duality?

Those who doubt the need to change quickly should talk to their customers, as the message is very clear. Customers now expect a consistent and high quality digital experience in everything that they do.

Entrepreneurial success today in the area of Digital technology and analytics comes from three key areas: digital enterprise, data analytics and security, and privacy. Perhaps more than any other of the EY 7 Drivers of Growth, the Digital driver underpins and connects with each and every other one. People work remotely because of digital technology and communications; customers order online and pay for goods and services with an ever-expanding range of digital payment systems; supply chain and operational efficiency is transformed by new technologies such as 3D printing and digital shipping methods; risk is both managed and increased through the adoption of digital security systems.

"Technology is changing so quickly that it is hard for me to keep up to date," confesses Michael Wu of Maxim Group. "My vision for Maxim's is we need to become Maxim's 4.0. We are now experimenting with drone delivery, robotics, 3D printing, and manufacturing 4.0. The message I give to my staff is that the world is moving forward rapidly and change is going to happen sooner than we think."

Manny Stul of Moose Toys was one of the first toy company CEOs to create content for the then nascent YouTube. "Children love storytelling and we seized the opportunity to integrate branded content such as webisodes while supporting the small but growing channels that were 'unboxing' their toys to share with their fans," he says. "Today we continue to explore, test, learn, and amplify our digital relationship with our customer base. The fluid nature of key digital channels such as YouTube also allows our audience to help shape future product lines based on their feedback, comments, and character preferences."

Digital enterprise

Many of the Entrepreneurs, as part of their focus on accelerating the growth of their companies, already have digital at the heart of the way they do business and are applying digital thinking to drive innovation throughout every aspect of it.

"To give you a life example, India demonetized 85% of its currency on November 8, 2016. So, we immediately huddled together and said, 'Hey, this is going to change the way we do business,'" remembers Uday Kotak of Kotak Mahindra Bank. "Within a period of close to five months, we created a new digital account called 811 (which is the date on which India demonetized), which we introduced in March 2017. The 811 account enables customers to open a full bank account on mobile in three minutes flat. We went all out to build something out of a sense of paranoia, and 811 has been one of our most significant success stories – all grown from our customer base."

Digital transformation isn't restricted to financial services or retail. "I think the next disruption that is occurring is the digitization of agriculture," says Murad Al-Katib of AGT Food and Ingredients Inc. "Under the system today, we plant crops around the world and try to monitor those crops and predict [crop yields]. With changes that are happening now, drones will fly over our farmland, satellite imagery will track the vegetable growth, and large farm equipment manufacturers are tracking (with GPS) seed placement, fertilizer placement, inoculant, seeding, and harvest rates.

"By capturing this big data and inputting it into an analytic system, predictive analytics will be able to provide more information on supply chain. By then layering in blockchain on food security, the agricultural industries of 5 or 10 years from now won't resemble the industry we have today."

Fellow food grower Rosario Bazán of DanPer agrees. "With drones we can make observations on the general situations of our fields. Right now, we are developing a project using satellite technology to determine the status of every square meter of the largest sections of cultivated land that we have. We are developing this project with a U.K. university and it's a unique and exclusive project, because through the satellite we will be capturing all the different variables that tell us how the crops are doing and what we need to do to increase the yield and decrease costs."

In response to their need for continual innovation, successful entrepreneurs and the leaders of large corporations alike increasingly recognize the importance of actively building relationships with the innovation ecosystem. Partnering with start-ups and university departments can turbocharge the digital journey, giving you access to frontier technologies at an early stage of development.

One key trend we in EY see transforming our clients' businesses both large and small is industry convergence. Sector lines are blurring. The world's largest taxi service owns no cars and employs no drivers; the world's largest hotel chain owns no property and services no rooms. One day we may see a global distribution giant emerge that employs no truck drivers. They are digital innovators.

Consumers are generally living and working much longer; they have higher expectations of the pace, quality, and nature of the service they receive from the companies with which they do business.

Many of today's consumers also have a much stronger social conscience than ever before and make purchasing decisions accordingly. They are also better informed and readily communicate their experience of brands to each other in seconds across the world. We are all adjusting to major lifestyle changes that will be driven by technologies such as driverless cars, 3D printing, drones, robot caretakers, and AI. There has never been a time when such enormous opportunities have existed for innovative entrepreneurs.

"The pace of that change is now so incredible that it's almost impossible to keep up with it. I think you can get a competitive advantage if you are a prime mover – first with the idea and first to market," says Jim Nixon of Nixon Energy Investments.

Data and analytics

Twenty years ago businesses that led the technology revolution invested in hardware that gave them significant processing power. Ten years ago the focus had shifted to adoption of software systems that enabled them to harness the value of hardware.

Whether or not you agree with U.K. mathematician Clive Humby, who coined the phrase "data is the new oil," few would argue that a company's data is an increasing asset. The Entrepreneurs creatively capture, store, analyze, and harness data to optimize every aspect of their business. Our research shows that businesses that adopt analytics throughout their business outperform their competitors in both revenue and profit growth by 6% to 8%. Entrepreneurs at the EY World Entrepreneur Of

The Year 2018 event in Monaco predicted a further shift of power from those who own data to those who can use that data most effectively.

The EY World Entrepreneur Of The Year Alumni Social Impact Award 2018 winner, Andrew Forrest, CEO of Australia's Fortescue Metals, is but one example of an entrepreneur who is committed to harnessing the power of data analytics and artificial intelligence to make a quantum leap. Through his charitable foundation, Mindaroo, he is leading a major initiative (the Universal Cancer Databank) to establish a public, shared database of anonymized patient data for cancer sufferers globally. This is already accelerating the progress toward finding cures by making patient data more readily available to the research and treatment communities.

Security and privacy

We are living in a world that is becoming increasingly digital, and at an exponential rate. Customer and consumer data is becoming an increasingly valuable asset to both businesses and individuals. Newer businesses often have a competitive advantage at capturing and utilizing their data, as they are not encumbered by multiple, complex legacy systems that may not communicate with each other.

In this new world, protecting this valuable asset is a key priority. As James Snook, deputy director of the U.K.'s Office for Cyber Security, says, "My message for companies that think they haven't been attacked is: You're not looking hard enough." Highly sophisticated digital attacks need to be defended with dynamic and proactive controls. As customer data is frequently derived from multiple sources and often crosses functional and even corporate boundaries in the supply chain, this task is becoming highly complex.

Leading entrepreneurs build strong relationships across supply chains and develop strategies to protect data across them. Their privacy and screening policies, processes, and controls are fully aligned with customers and suppliers. Typically they are led from the top, not siloed into a risk role.

In summary, we can learn from our winning Entrepreneurs that early adopting new technologies throughout the business has a significant impact on each driver.

10

Driver #4: Operations

"From surviving to thriving"

om Peters, the great management thinker and writer, says "Leaders win through logistics. Vision, sure. Strategy, yes. But when you go to war, you need to have both toilet paper and bullets at the right place at the right time. In other words, you must win through superior logistics." Operations are all about the how of business.

As an entrepreneur accelerating the growth of your business, you're already focused on understanding your customers' needs and meeting them. Your operating model is the link between your strategic intent to satisfy these customer needs and the ability of your business to deliver on that intent (See Figure 10.1.). Successful entrepreneurs have a clear approach that aligns all components of operations and supply chain with their strategy.

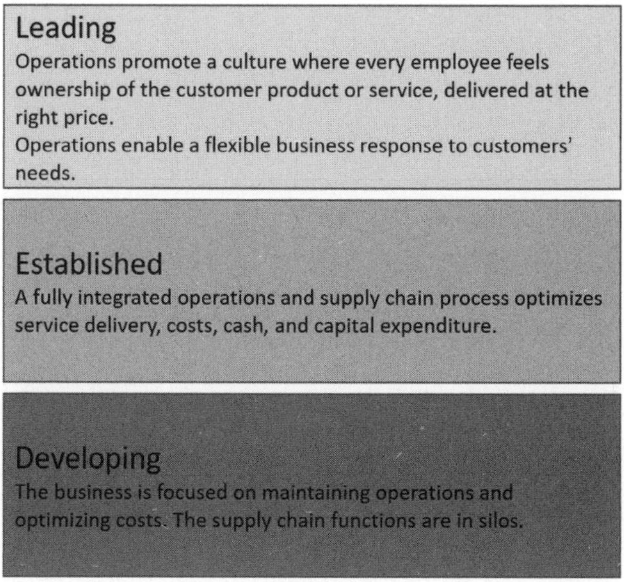

Leading
Operations promote a culture where every employee feels ownership of the customer product or service, delivered at the right price.
Operations enable a flexible business response to customers' needs.

Established
A fully integrated operations and supply chain process optimizes service delivery, costs, cash, and capital expenditure.

Developing
The business is focused on maintaining operations and optimizing costs. The supply chain functions are in silos.

FIGURE 10.1 EY 7 Drivers of Growth – Operations

Operations and supply chain management are never static. Successful entrepreneurs have to continually adjust supply chain elements to reflect changes in product mix, customer preferences, locations, distribution channels, supplier base, and technology developments to name a few. They leave nothing to chance, taking control by analyzing their operations and ensuring that all the links in their supply chain are aligned, making changes as and when needed.

Top-performing entrepreneurial companies effectively leverage supply chains to optimize costs and enable growth. They focus on achieving greater agility and responsiveness to deliver superior results. This means using machine learning to automate parts of the supply chain and predictive analytics to keep ahead of the growth curve for the business. Operational excellence today is increasingly about harnessing digital capabilities.

Our research shows that successful entrepreneurs focus on three aspects of operations:

1. Operations strategy
2. Operational excellence and continuous improvement
3. Operational resilience and sustainability

Operations strategy

A company's operating model is the link between its overall strategy and its ability to meet the needs of specific customers and stakeholders. In today's global business environment, operating strategies often need to be customized to various product, cost, and market requirements. In addition, the operating model needs to be aligned across functional silos and geographies within the enterprise and with external participants in the supply chain, and continuously monitored to ensure desired results.

Successful entrepreneurs have a clear understanding of their customer needs and are obsessive about creating customer value. They use this understanding to establish an initial operating strategy, knowing that this is a dynamic system that will evolve as the company accelerates growth and requirements change. They ensure that the strategy embraces an innovation culture that fully aligns the supply chain with distinct customer segments. Key elements they continually evaluate include:

- **How can operational excellence help accelerate growth?**
- **What are my core competencies?** What operations should the business handle in-house and what should be outsourced? Geography, capabilities, costs, and value will all play their part in deciding.
- **What are my core values?** What is critical to my business brand? How vital is it for me to commit to local economic development, to create jobs, to ensure my values are lived in every part of my operations?
- **What aspects of my business could be improved through external relationships?** Do I build or buy? Is speed to market a critical advantage? Could we manufacture with an expert vendor? Could we outsource administrative functions such as credit control or payroll to achieve cost reductions?
- **How do I ensure my business culture extends to every part of my supply chain, including those elements handled externally?** Can I ensure that my suppliers' staff are fairly paid and have decent working conditions? How will we guarantee quality?
- **How do I ensure that all of my back office processes are as efficient as possible to minimize costs without compromising on our promise to customers?**

The winning Entrepreneurs have successfully built a number of businesses, taking them from developing through established and ultimately to leading. As they grow these companies, their operations and supply chain strategies necessarily change to scale effectively. Not all will adopt the same strategy to meet growth challenges. While some form close strategic partnerships and alliances to ensure resilience in their supply chain – others, such as Murad Al-Katib at AGT Food and Ingredients, grow to own more of their supply chain through strategic acquisitions.

"You have also got to implement systems and processes that are self-sustaining, and for most businesses, that is kind of difficult," says Jim Nixon of Nixon Energy Investments. "We don't like talking about systems and processes; we like doing things. You must make sure you have backfilled with the expertise and have the capability to build those systems and processes to where you have a business that is self-sustaining. At that stage your key imperative needs to be keeping people focused on the ball and moving forward. The last thing you want to be doing is running a business based on firefighting because the structure has not changed."

Fifteen years ago, Maxim Group was exclusively focused on Hong Kong. Now the group has stores in mainland China and Southeast Asia. But with this overseas expansion comes challenges. "Quality control is the most difficult and important part of a food and beverage business," says Michael Wu, Maxim Group's CEO. "If you have to control the food and service quality in 20 cities, the challenges of operating in those 20 cities versus one city are very different. So, while there are many opportunities, I always have my checks and balances to ensure that we expand in a measured and disciplined way and that our culture is intact. Wherever we expand – whether it's in coffee, burgers, sushi, or dim sum – our team must embrace our values and culture."

Entrepreneurs on a high-growth trajectory need to evaluate where to add scale – in the areas of people, process, and technology. They adjust their operating strategy and style to reflect the realities of accelerated growth. Our winning Entrepreneurs recognize they will need to change their management style from making every key decision to letting others share that autonomy. "I like to delegate to my people and make them accountable by giving them authority to make their own decisions," says Wu.

Exceptional entrepreneurs understand when to say "no" to opportunities in order to have the time and resources to say "yes" to others. The late Steve Jobs, founder of Apple Inc., says, "It's only by saying 'no' that you can concentrate on the things that are really important."[1] Saying "no" involves an ability to be ruthless in the pursuit of that ultimate growth target.

"In late 2011, we took the bold step of abandoning every project the company was working on and bet everything on a mobile tablet-only strategy. This meant 'killing' games with hundreds of thousands of users on Facebook and dedicating every resource to new projects," says Ilkka Paananen of Finnish games developer Supercell. "The strategy worked well."

Operational excellence and continuous improvement

Leading entrepreneurs effectively manage operations at both the macro and micro levels. They see the big picture opportunities, such as adapting their supply chain to changing customer behaviors, as well as being able to focus on more tactical areas. Their primary focus is on processes that have a direct impact on

---

[1] *BusinessWeek*, 2004.

customer value, but they extend this thinking to all processes and functions in the business. They drive a culture where even those who work in back office or support functions such as HR, risk, and finance understand that, ultimately, they are there to create customer value. By having this broad view, the Entrepreneurs are able to achieve greater agility and responsiveness in the marketplace, often leading to greater revenue growth and lower costs than their competitors.

An essential part of operational excellence and continuous improvement is identifying and measuring the important metrics that determine success. Once you identify how to measure operational success you can use a number of technologies to collect and analyze the supporting data – an ERP system, blockchain, IoT devices, customer satisfaction survey results, and cost ratios. Through the increasing power of data analytics and artificial intelligence, company leaders have better visibility of these metrics than ever before. New people with the necessary skills, such as data scientists, are needed to realize the full potential of these new sources of information.

Sometimes it is useful to adopt benchmarking to measure how well your operations are supporting the business. Examples might include:

- Abandoned baskets on ecommerce sites
- Occupancy levels in a hotel
- Revenue by passenger miles for an airline
- Production volume within established quality standards for a manufacturer
- Customer satisfaction and net promoter scores
- Adherence to various budget and financial measures
- Lead times – speed to market
- Average shipping days

As industry convergence is rapidly blurring sector boundaries, opportunities for benchmarking across industries can lead to transformational improvements. Consider this example from the energy services industry. "We have an environment that is rather dangerous. We have people on the rig floor with chains that spin, men working with heavy equipment. There is a very strong move towards robotic utilization and automatic guidance systems," says Jim Nixon of Nixon Energy Investments. "So, if you look at drilling 20 years ago, it was an agricultural-type industry. Now we are bringing aerospace technology and digitalization into the industry to remove people from harm's way. The level of jobs that are coming are interesting because they are very high tech around automation of what the previous process was. I think it will not be long before you have someone sitting in an office in Houston guiding a well bore in Malaysia – I don't think that's more than a few years away."

Deciding on the optimum locus of decision making and responsibility for operational excellence and continuous improvement is a hallmark of effective leadership. The winning Entrepreneurs ensure that many decisions are distributed and made by local managers or functional leads who are closer to the customer and other aspects of the supply chain. "Supercell was founded on the idea that the company's management should focus on finding the best people, create a culture that enables them to do what they do best, and then get out of the way so they can get on with it ... ," says Ilkka Paananen of Supercell. "In order to get the most from my staff, I strive to minimize bureaucracy. This maximizes the time people can spend on their work."

Jack Welch, the legendary onetime CEO of GE, famously said, "Speed is everything. It is the indispensable ingredient of competitiveness."[2] But achieving speed as your business grows

---

[2] "25 Lessons from Jack Welch," LinkedIn Pulse, May 31, 2016.

and becomes inevitably more complex is not a simple game. "The trouble is that as you get bigger you get more structured. The more structured you get, the more systems you put in place, and the more systems you have the slower you get," explains Manny Stul of Moose Toys. "Surrounding yourself with very high-quality people, ensuring innovation and disruption on every level – both improving your product and the way you operate – enables you to constantly improve and adjust, especially in this very fast-paced environment.... The world is changing so quickly that if you are not up to speed you are going to be crucified."

Operational resilience and sustainability

Operational resilience is all about minimizing risk, whether from supply shortages due to breakdowns, labor shutdowns, government protectionism and trade barriers, or natural disasters. Leading companies focus on developing an overall risk, resilience, and sustainability strategy that answers the question, What if? What if my key supplier goes to the wall? What if a hurricane hits our factory in the Philippines? What if our key market suddenly introduces a 25% tariff on my goods?

The lesson we can learn from winning Entrepreneurs can be summarized as: a chain is only as good as the weakest link. So how do you strengthen your supply chain and make it sufficiently resilient to respond quickly to unanticipated changes and failures?

Strengthening operational resilience might include evaluating whether you should bring critical elements in-house, ensuring there are alternatives to your current supply chain partners, or building in redundancy in the event of a temporary or permanent break in the chain.

The Swedish flatpacked furniture company IKEA is renowned for stocking over 9,500 products in each of its stores. It buys from 1,800 suppliers in 50 countries around the world. To do this successfully it has developed a proprietary inventory system that monitors stock movement every day and automatically orders for restocking overnight. Flatpacked furniture takes much less warehouse space to store. IKEA's customers choose, load, and assemble the furniture themselves, reducing significant costs. IKEA passes on these savings to its customers, creating a virtuous cycle of demand and supply.

As we have seen, in some circumstances, winning Entrepreneurs build sustainable operations by owning more of the supply chain than their competitors. For Murad Al-Katib, who is in the pulse crop business, selectively owning rail lines and tidewater access became a competitive advantage.

Perhaps two of the most important aspects of external supply chain management are trust and relationships. But how do you check the quality and trustworthiness of supply chain relationships? References; small test pilots of small runs or projects; clear agreements with specific criteria built-in; and good, two-way communication are all useful. Not only do these relationships build strength in your existing business – sometimes they lead to major upticks in your growth too. "Due to the professional reputations and the high-quality relationships we had built up over years, we were able to obtain ZEJULA from Merck during the first stage of human testing," say Lonnie Moulder and Mary Lynne Hedley, cofounders of cancer therapy company TESARO, Inc. "Despite being much smaller than many other companies vying for this product, Merck believed TESARO could advance the development and commercialization more quickly than anyone else."

It was only when Manny Stul had a supply chain issue that nearly cost him the company – a contract manufacturer that used inappropriate products for the toys they were making – that he discovered the weak link in his own supply chain. In this case, trust in his supplier had been misplaced. However, because of the trust and relationships that he had nurtured with other suppliers, retailers, and customers over many years, he drew back from the brink of disaster to save the company and go on to great success with Moose Toys. Sometimes you can only learn the hard way about just how resilient your supply chain is.

Purpose and social responsibility

Purpose and social responsibility are no longer a paragraph in the annual report: they have to underlie every part of the business in an authentic way. Customers, stakeholders, and regulators expect responsible capitalism, whether safe working conditions, fair pay, low carbon footprint, responsible use of resources, or sustainable practices. And today, social responsibility needs to extend to every part of the supply chain.

Few of us will forget the images of young children working in dark sweatshops stitching a famous sportswear brand's footballs. The company didn't employ the children but the reputational damage was as severe as if it had. With social media, it is impossible to hide irresponsible practices from view, and customers will and do repay lapses by going elsewhere.

"In Peru there was a high percentage of poverty all around and I understood that one of the ways to reduce poverty in our country in a structured way was to generate jobs, jobs with dignity, and to generate jobs visibly," says Rosario Bazán of DanPer. "We needed to build a company that was sustainable and focused on quality, not just caring for the quality of our product, but caring as well for the quality relationships with our workers, suppliers, and investors. Building an ethical, successful, and world-renowned company was the most effective way of contributing to Peru's national development and the alleviation of poverty.... More than 20 years ago, when we launched DanPer, the term 'social responsibility' had yet to be coined. But we already understood that respecting and treating our workers well, promoting their development, being fair to our clients and suppliers, and looking after the environment were fundamental to making our company sustainably profitable."

Winning Entrepreneurs unilaterally have a purpose that goes beyond profit. For some, they extend their influence into the field of public policy, showing that private enterprise can work effectively with governments to effect social change. "The government financial programs for this [housing] segment kept evolving during the years," says Rubens Menin of MRV Engenharia in Brazil. "And private companies always participated in discussion forums to optimize the processes. The new government housing program called 'My House, My Life' uses the resources of the FGTS (fund for employees), and it was implemented in 2008 by the Federal Government in partnership with a group of private companies including MRV." By making a high-end bet on low-income families, Menin's company has built some 300,000 homes in a country dogged by housing shortages.

The Entrepreneurs know that challenges may be around every corner, and that they need to be both good at anticipating them and agile enough to withstand unforeseeable shocks. As Napoleon said, "The amateurs discuss tactics; the professionals discuss logistics."

11

Driver #5: Funding and Finance

"Failing to plan is planning to fail"

T here comes a moment in every company's life when funding is needed to realize growth potential. As Richard Harroch, managing director of venture capital firm VantagePoint, says, "It's almost always harder to raise capital than you thought it would be, and it always takes longer. So plan for that ..."[1]

Our research shows (see Figure 11.1) that entrepreneurs who succeed in driving growth focus on five key areas in Funding and Finance, and this focus changes as the company evolves from Developing to Leading.

Leading
Finance is a strategic business partner, supporting decisions to maximize return on capital.

Established
Leadership drives financial discipline to support growth and maintain access to capital.

Developing
The business is focused on establishing trust and financial credibility with key stakeholders.

FIGURE 11.1   EY 7 Drivers of Growth–Funding and finance

The five areas include:

1. *Appropriate funding* – sourcing the best-fit types of debt and equity capital from the right lenders and investors, in the appropriate amounts and proportions, at the right time

---

[1] "50 Inspirational Quotes For Startups And Entrepreneurs," Forbes, February 10, 2014.

2. *Effective finance team and organizational structure* – given the development stage of the business, to be able to plan financing needs, effectively manage cash flow, and provide company leadership with reliable information and metrics to run the business

3. *Finance processes and controls* – ensuring accurate and timely information is collected; having the right checks and balances in place that can provide an early warning of potential threats as well as robust systems for budgeting, credit, and cost control

4. *Data and technology* – enable smooth operation of the finance processes and controls described above

5. *Stakeholder management* – communicating the funding and finance state of the business to shareholders, lenders, regulators, and other government authorities, suppliers, customers, and employees

Leading companies focus on developing and executing a detailed funding strategy and capital allocation plan as they begin to work on major developmental milestones. These may include new product and service innovation, customer/market development, sales and marketing drives, key hires, working capital, or acquisitions.

Whether you raise venture capital, private equity funding, or decide to go public, one important consideration will be tax. Every structural decision you make, whatever group structure you adopt as the business gets more complex, how and where you accrue operating profits – all these affect the way your company is taxed.

"Tax planning is essential for success in this changing regulatory tax environment," advises James Markham, EY Global Leader for Growth Markets – Tax. "High-growth companies are differentiated from peers by using forward-thinking tax planning.

The changing regulatory environment requires current knowledge of megatrends. Proper tax planning should be considered by high-growth entrepreneurs in each of the growth drivers – tax permeates structuring deals with customers, compensation plans for talent, operations and supply chain design, decisions on where and how to obtain necessary funding and finance, and how to structure game-changing transactions and alliances."

"Small businesses don't fail for lack of capital," admonishes Mark Cuban, serial entrepreneur and star of *Shark Tank*. "They fail for lack of brains."[2]

Leading entrepreneurs demonstrate that success in funding and finance is an ongoing process: calculating how much the business will need for different purposes; identifying when the business will need the funds (using cash flow modeling); plotting significant performance milestones that are likely to drive value inflections; evaluating different financing alternatives and their sources; and obtaining the funding.

Funding growth

Few entrepreneurial companies who are really accelerating their growth are able to fund that growth entirely from internally generated cash flow (sales and profit) – most will need to access external capital from equity investors and lenders. The types of available finance changes as the company matures, eventually moving from soft loans from family and friends to venture capital/private equity and public markets.

As entrepreneurial companies grow, they generally require larger capital raises and may consider either raising substantial amounts of private equity or an initial public offering (IPO).

---

[2] "Mark Cuban's Advice on Starting a Small Business," *Capitalist Creations*, August 7, 2014.

Our research, and insights from the Entrepreneurs we interviewed, show it is wise to adopt the disciplines of being a public company before actually becoming public. This creates value from an investor perspective and prepares company management for the rigor and requirements of large private equity and public market investors.

"From a very early stage we started acting like we were a public company," says Jim Nixon of Nixon Energy Investments. "We did all the compliance, reporting, and accounting the right way. We did investor updates. We did almost everything inside the company as though we were public. The objective was to get to the stage where we would float the company and take it public. About two years before the last transaction it became apparent to me that there are multiple ways of going public. My blinkered view of it was that we needed to float the company, but the other way was to build up a private enterprise that is acquired by a public company. That way the business goes public, so that's eventually what we did and over a period of time we built toward that public exit. We took on some public debt as a kind of precursor to a public offering and that raised our profile in the industry … then someone made a compelling offer with public company multiples to absorb us into their much larger publicly traded company. So, I think it's important to be open-minded."

The process of raising capital can be exhausting and time-consuming for the CEO and for the leadership team. Adequate lead time for planning and executing the capital raising process is always recommended. We found that our award-winning Entrepreneurs were able to see their business from the perspective of an investor, to understand how companies are valued, and also to develop a compelling corporate story that explained their vision for the business. They were also quick to involve external advisors and their board for help in determining how best to present the business in a compelling way.

Growth story

"I have always been fascinated by the intersection between storytelling and entrepreneurship," says Richard Branson, founder and CEO of Virgin. "We would be nothing without our story."[3] Storytelling is a critical weapon in the armory of every successful entrepreneur. Tailored to the needs of various stakeholders (shareholders, lenders, potential customers, and employees), the growth story brings the history, performance, vision, and execution plans of the business to life. Above all else, investors, in particular, are keen to know that leaders can deliver against their plans. The growth story needs to be both ambitious and achievable and should be a vehicle for demonstrating the leadership team's ability to meet its targets (see Figure 11.2).

Determine how much you need for different purposes

Determining how much you need and when you need it (typically derived from the cash flow forecast) and setting key milestones are interdependent, so think of them in conjunction with each other. Begin by picking a time horizon – say, 18 to 24 months – and then identify what significant milestones are likely to be completed in that time frame. Milestones are proof points that build trust in your ability to meet targets.

The value investors place on your company will be based, in large part, on your track record of meeting growth targets married to the scale of your ambition. The higher the valuation is – or is likely to be – the less equity dilution that you will need to bear (i.e., the smaller the percentage of equity in the business that will be issued to investors for a given amount raised).

---

[3] https://www.virgin.com/richard-branson/why-entrepreneurs-are-storytellers.

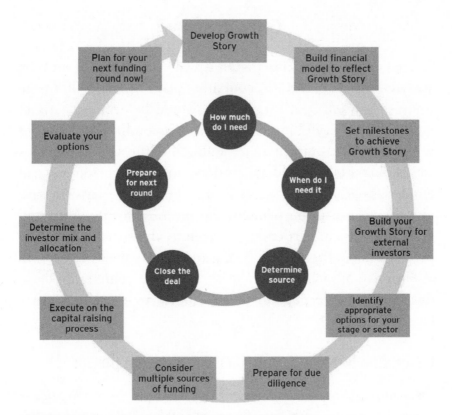

FIGURE 11.2   Funding growth – key steps

Identifying when you will need the funds

Timing capital needs is important. Raise capital for too short a period and you may not have time to complete the milestones you intended; leave it too late and you may leave yourself cash poor and exposed.

"How do you determine the speed of growth?" asks Mohed Altrad of The Altrad Group. "It's a trade-off between dilution of capital and growth. When your company is doing well, it attracts investors, so the money is there – and then you have to negotiate with your investors if you want to keep control – not lose your shareholding. To do that your group has to generate a lot of free cash flow."

Determining the speed of growth is more than just a funding issue. It will impact almost all the other drivers of growth too: talent, operations, technology, and risk, for example. Linda Hasenfratz of Canadian automotive parts company Linamar Corporation says, "We are not trying to grow at 99%. I would rather grow between 10% and 20% a year, not just because that means that you can cash flow your growth but because that sort of consistent sustainable growth means that you can also create the people that you need. It's not just about cash. It's about having the right people with the right skills and leadership capabilities to allow us to continue to grow. You can only grow your human capital at a certain rate, just like your financial capital."

Evaluating different capital alternatives and where to source them

In addition to anticipating the timing of certain milestones, the Entrepreneurs we interviewed carefully consider the types of financing that are most appropriate for them. They think about funding sources at the different stages of development, as well as the use or purpose of the fund raise.

Financing options include bank loans, leasing, government grants and loans, equity investment from angels, venture capital, private equity or strategic partners (who can typically bring much more than just capital), and, ultimately, public markets.

Entrepreneurs generally use debt financing as a funding source when their companies have assets that the lender can use to collateralize the loan(s). These may include working capital related items (such as accounts receivable and inventory, which can support shorter-term lines of credit) or fixed assets such as real estate and equipment (which can generally be funded – in part at least – by loans with longer repayment terms). Each funding source has its advantages and disadvantages. Banks will often insist on the business owner providing personal guarantees (with personal risk), particularly if the company is young.

When the need for funds is partially driven by expansion into new geographical markets, entrepreneurs also consider whether the expansion funding should come from the domestic market (where they are based) or from the targeted international expansion markets (where they intend to expand) or some combination of the two. Factors to consider include the cost and availability of capital in each geography; location of any assets that are serving as collateral for loans; and local regulations that will impact funding, taxation, and repatriation of funds (exchange controls).

Often, funding comes from some form of equity financing. Equity investors, such as venture capitalists, may seek representation on the investee company board of directors. If the right investors are selected, their involvement in the company can add real value by making vital introductions and providing relevant expertise. You never quite know where the right investment partner can lead you.

"I realized that while I had a great idea, a good education, and passion, I also needed strategic partners who could bring operations experience and provide funding," recalls Murad Al-Katib of AGT Food and Ingredients. "I identified Arbel, a Turkish company owned by the Arslan family. They were experienced lentil processors and were prepared to invest US$1 million in my embryonic company. Not only did AGT become viable, but six years later I bought the Arslan's family business for US$104 million."

Being prepared to dilute your shareholding comes with the territory of equity finance. "My advice on capital is always 'don't be greedy.' Be willing to share," says Jim Nixon.

Finding suitable investors is very much like finding suitable suppliers: ask trusted peers, advisors, and professional advisors for recommendations. Advisors can also help align capital sources with the long-term goals of the business. This is likely to lead to a successful marriage of investor and investee.

As in the choice of a spouse, you should spend time selecting the right investor. "Take your time and don't rush into a private equity partnership," advises Jim Nixon. "Private equity people are good salespeople. They will tell everyone that they are the best private equity firm in the world but when the rubber meets the road – when you talk to others they have invested in – you understand how they were treated, how fair they have been, and how they have handled problems and road bumps."

While the focus is on growth and the sunny upsides of your growth trajectory, the fact is every entrepreneurial journey has its challenging moments. "You need partners who are with you when things are tough," says Dame Rosemary Squire of Trafalgar Entertainment Group, "and you are in the trenches fighting because in all businesses you have bad times and you need to be able to weather the storm and not be too short term in your thinking. It's very unfashionable these days to take a longer-term view, but our founding investors did that. Because of their long-term view, we ultimately sold to private equity and then we sold again a second time to private equity."

People and organization for an effective finance function

While all entrepreneurs should be financially savvy from the get-go, as the company grows, so will the needs of your finance function. Typically the team will need to manage compliance and risk as well as providing transparent data on the company's performance. Finance heads will increasingly become a strategic partner in the business.

Hiring, retaining, and developing people with the necessary finance skills and competencies are critical to the success of the business.

You may have started out with an in-house controller rather than an experienced CFO, but as soon as you want to raise funds formally you'll need someone who can talk to investors and stakeholders. When you decide to bring on board a CFO will depend on budget, growth ambitions, and your overall plans for building your senior management team.

Selecting someone with complementary skills to your own is an excellent way to balance the team and give each of you distinct roles to play in the development of the company. Choosing someone who is not just a superstar with spreadsheets but a good communicator and strategic thinker will help you accelerate your growth plans.

Finance processes and controls for an effective finance function

Establishing controls and the basis for good financial information from the beginning is an example of how our winning Entrepreneurs stand out from competitors. Early disciplines and controls aren't only essential to prevent fraud or theft but they help validate your corporate story. However, the Entrepreneurs balance the need for controls and the need for agility.

"We are always trying to streamline processes, because the problem is that there is no shortage of people who want to add procedures, approvals, and bureaucracy," says Linda Hasenfratz of Linamar Corporation. "But I think it's our job as leaders to push back on that and say, 'why do we need that?' We need to rely on our people to make good decisions; they shouldn't have to be told how to do every last thing."

Data and technology for an effective finance function

Financial systems run on data and technology and have clear interdependence with the Digital and Technology driver. The finance function needs to select and optimize stage-appropriate enterprise resource planning (ERP) systems that provide the desired reports to inform management and stakeholders of the company's financial position.

Stakeholder management

The number of stakeholders a company needs to manage increases with size. They include shareholders, lenders, customers, suppliers, employees, board members, regulators, local communities, and, over time, policy makers. Managing the different information needs of these stakeholder groups can prove challenging. Leading companies manage these important relationships by identifying key stakeholders, customizing relevant messages and clear communications, and managing stakeholder expectations.

"The best advice I can give around raising capital is that you need to be very clear and report regularly and be transparent," advises Dame Rosemary Squire of Trafalgar Entertainment Group. "I think high quality information for your shareholders and business partners is essential."

When you lead a public company, stakeholder management becomes even more important – and complex. As Olivia Lum of desalinization company Hyflux Ltd. explains, "You must often explain to shareholders who might not understand your strategy."

In summary, the Funding and Finance driver is critical for sustainable growth. Our winning Entrepreneurs demonstrate the importance of having a clear vision of the ambition together with milestones along the way; they understand the need to invest in people, processes, and technology to operate a robust finance function; and finally they focus on being able to communicate their unique growth story to all their stakeholders.

12

Driver #6: Transactions and Alliances

"Right transaction, right price, right time"

There's an old proverb that goes "Fools build houses, and wise men buy them." When it comes to deciding whether to build or buy in the context of accelerating entrepreneurial growth, it's more complex and nuanced (see Figure 12.1). Transactions and alliances are almost always part of any exceptional business growth story; the question is deciding when and where to adopt them – and then with whom.

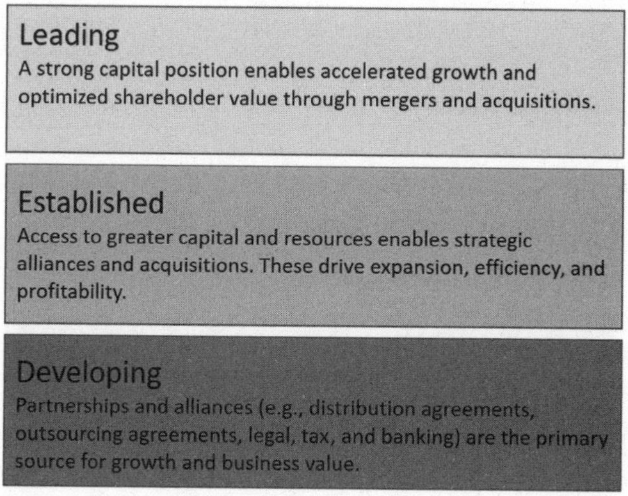

Leading
A strong capital position enables accelerated growth and optimized shareholder value through mergers and acquisitions.

Established
Access to greater capital and resources enables strategic alliances and acquisitions. These drive expansion, efficiency, and profitability.

Developing
Partnerships and alliances (e.g., distribution agreements, outsourcing agreements, legal, tax, and banking) are the primary source for growth and business value.

FIGURE 12.1   EY 7 Drivers of Growth – Transactions and alliances

Your company's growth is likely to follow a combination of the approaches depicted in the simple matrix shown in Figure 12.2. Growth can be achieved by:

- Selling more *existing* products and services to *existing* customers
- Selling *new* products and services to *existing* customers

- Selling *existing* products and services to *new* customers
- Selling *new* products and services to *new* customers.

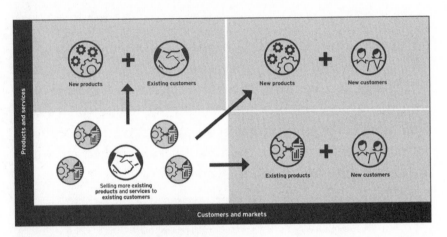

FIGURE 12.2 Growth options

The exceptional Entrepreneurs we interviewed have accelerated the growth of their businesses by using a well-planned combination of organic growth (growing both their customer and product base using existing and directly hired resources) and inorganic growth (growing products or customers in new markets through acquisitions or strategic alliances).

"Transactions and alliances are one of the best ways for high-growth entrepreneurs to access new customers, products, and markets – done properly, they can be transformative for entrepreneurial businesses," says Kath Carter, EY Global Leader, Growth Markets Transaction Advisory Services.

Sector convergence, globalization, and innovative cognitive technologies are driving new opportunities for entrepreneurs to turbocharge their growth through alliances and partnerships. Moreover, big market leaders are hungry to participate in the ideas and innovations generated by entrepreneurial companies – more than ever before. The pace of change favors the fast, and inorganic growth can offer a shortcut to new market opportunities.

Our exceptional Entrepreneurs show that pacing growth is critical. Not only do you need to ensure you have the organizational capacity to support a sudden growth surge, but you may also be allocating capital and resources to integrate an acquisition into your current operation. The Entrepreneurs have also built capacity to take advantage of an unforeseen opportunity as it arises. Not all strategic transactions are offensive; sometimes they are defensive moves to prevent an existing or prospective competitor from gaining competitive advantage.

Sourcing potential investee companies can derive from anywhere in a company's ecosystem of contacts. Mohed Altrad of The Altrad Group made it known that he was interested in finding suitable companies to form part of his group. "You start to identify common interests and finally you can purchase them because it's in the interest of both parties," he says. Altrad ensured every business interaction was a potential route to finding acquisitions – exhibitions, conferences, and meetings with his bank. "In the beginning you don't have much confidence but slowly you acquire that, and you acquire trust from all the people in your environment," he says.

While inorganic growth is simple in concept, it can be difficult to execute successfully.

Entrepreneurial success in the area of Transactions and alliances rests on getting three critical elements right:

1. *Transaction strategy and planning* – the what, when, and why of what you need to accelerate the growth of your business
2. *Acquisitions, partnerships, and alliances* – which capability do you need to own in-house and what could you access through an acquisition, partnership, or strategic alliance arrangement

3. *Transaction effectiveness* – how to make a transaction work, from sourcing through integration to realizing the intended synergies and value, while keeping current operations unaffected.

Transaction strategy and planning

Inorganic growth is often used to fill gaps in your capabilities, geographic footprint, or business portfolio. These may include:

- New products and services
- Innovations that will enhance or extend intellectual property (IP)
- New geographies/markets
- Strong pools of talent (sometimes called acquihires)
- Resilience, sustainability, or efficiency in the supply chain
- Scale to achieve greater brand recognition, prepare the company for an IPO, financing, or acquisition by a larger company.

As a group, these exceptional Entrepreneurs have engineered hundreds of successful transactions and alliances – developing their own approaches to identifying and nurturing potential acquisitions, partnerships, and alliances. They have let it be known that they are acquisitive and are good to work with.

"Every time we have been successful on a transformation or deal," says Dame Rosemary Squire of Trafalgar Entertainment Group, "it's because we hung in there and we were ready to jump. It's all about communications – it's all about driving the team, having a team to bring with you, making sure your due diligence is thorough, looking at every angle of it – and doing that gave us a great position when the moment arose."

In many cases strategic transactions have catapulted the Entrepreneurs forward in a transformational way: Murad Al-Katib with Arbel; Rosario Bazán with her Danish partner, Arne Hensel Berg; Uday Kotak and Goldman Sachs; and Michael Wu with Starbucks and numerous other western franchises.

AGT's success is to a large extent based on an appetite for acquisitions. In 16 years it has acquired 17 companies and retained 16 of the management teams. When asked how he navigated all these transactions, Murad Al-Katib cites the example of the acquisition of his short-line railway. "The previous owner is a brilliant constructor of infrastructure, but he couldn't necessarily manage the whole business," he says. "So I put in place strong capital budgeting – so I can control his costs, but let him be innovative and let him build infrastructure that's world class and efficient. It's been two years since the acquisition and today I feel better about the management team than the day I bought them. That's the ultimate success in acquisition."

Realizing the benefits of these transformational transactions and alliances means recognizing that doing the deal is not the end of the journey – it is one step in the journey. Successful entrepreneurs will have conducted as much operational due diligence as financial diligence, as both have a major impact on the outcome of the venture. For example, a cultural alignment at all levels of the business is critical to post-deal retention, as is consideration of reward and incentive structures for key individuals with both the acquirer and the target. Having done the deal, a well-constructed and well-communicated post-merger integration plan is essential to success. Such plans typically include a Day 1 plan that would deal with leadership and management roles to remove uncertainty, and then cover the first 100 days.

Finally, there should always be a robust plan to ensure that business as usual continues uninterrupted and the core business does not flounder while the eyes of the leaders are focused on the acquisition.

International expansion

All successful entrepreneurs, even those operating in large established markets, agree that eventually a company must enter new geographic markets to achieve market leadership. It's impossible to think of a true market-leading brand that doesn't operate in multiple countries.

The Entrepreneurs consider a variety of questions before accelerating their growth through international expansion. Digital connectedness has brought the world closer together, but regulation, culture, and physical distance can still place roadblocks along the route:

- Which international markets do I prioritize?
- What is the best way for me to enter those markets: organically or by acquiring or partnering with a local player?
- What are the legal risks, cultural hazards, and market conditions that exist in the intended market?
- Is there adequate infrastructure to support the minimum requirements for my businesses (e.g., broadband and transport infrastructure, good local governance, communication systems)?

As Michael Wu of Maxim Group points out, strategic partners "can add tremendous value in terms of governance and strategy." In Maxim's case, they "have given very sound advice on our expansions into China and Southeast Asia," he says.

As shown in Figure 12.3, when deciding where to expand, you need to assess the size of the market opportunity, ease of doing business (language, local legal structures, time differences, and distance from home office), and local competition. Taking a comprehensive approach – coupled with reliable data and

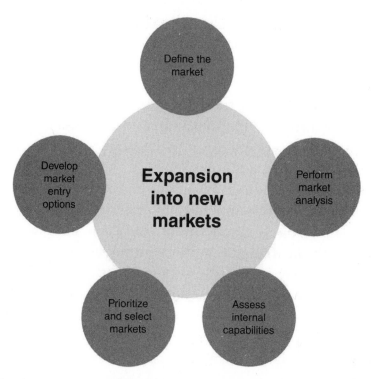

FIGURE 12.3   Key steps for successful market expansion

information – helps get to a solid shortlist. It may make sense to test your first leap overseas in a smaller, lower-risk environment before launching into a sizeable expansion market. That way you can test your assumptions, course correct, and refine your international strategy before the big leap.

The Entrepreneurs show us how to develop a market entry strategy from a range of options: direct exporting, franchising, licensing, partnering, acquisitions, building on a successful local product range, and green-field investment – building a facility from the ground up. There's no one-size-fits-all solution – each has its own benefits and risks – but applying some "what if" scenario planning to the process helps maximize the likelihood of success.

"We really had to look at the totality of the geopolitical environment," says Murad Al-Katib of AGT. "A lot of businesses don't recognize the geopolitical sensitivities of the countries that they are dealing in."

Partnerships and alliances

In addition to mergers and acquisitions, the Entrepreneurs we interviewed show how strategic partnerships and alliances can expand a business portfolio and/or reach new markets. These alliances can often help deliver increased scale or unique capabilities to help create competitive differentiation. Some partnerships and alliances contribute new products, services, platforms, or an ability to better access new geographies.

Sometimes the association with a recognized brand or market leader can add to an entrepreneurial company's reputation. "We ended up doing a deal with Time Warner, TCI, Ameritech, and Bell Atlantic – four giant American companies, two media companies, two telecommunication companies," says Craig Heatley of Rainbow Corporation and SKY TV. "They came in for half of the business in 1991, paying US$108 million. It was a win-win. This deal allowed us to stop putting our own money in and gave the business a seal of approval in the public eye because suddenly people were saying, 'Oh, okay, well if these people are investing in this company then it must be for real. Maybe we should become a subscriber.'"

In a partnership or alliance, unlike an acquisition, decision making is shared and not fully controlled by any one partner. It is, therefore, particularly important to clarify needs and objectives, select the right partners, decide on the optimum structure and term, and determine success criteria. As with any business relationship, you should also have a plan if things don't work out as hoped. Can you exit smoothly?

"Partnerships are like a marriage – there are marriages that work for a while and then they don't," says Craig Heatley. "There are marriages that should never have happened in the first place, and I would say partnerships are no different. Partnerships are just people with strengths and weaknesses, and sometimes you get it right and sometimes you get it wrong."

What are my needs and objectives?

Clearly articulating what you want to achieve out of a partnership or alliance is the first step to success, as well as choosing a partner that offers different but equal skills. "In my opinion the best partnerships are ones where you have complementary skills," advises Craig Heatley, "where one person is competent in one area, and another person is competent in another. The ones where the skills are similar, but where one may be dominant or whatever, that can give rise to bruised egos and those are the ones less likely to succeed."

How do I select the best partners?

Choosing business partners is an art as well as a science. "When you find a partner, it's very important that your values are aligned," says Michael Wu of Maxim's. "For example, if your partner's sole focus is on financial return, you are going to have to execute and act in a manner that delivers rapid growth, often at the expense of quality. If your partner's priorities are about creating and building a long-term brand and business, then that is very different. If you want to deliver quality, you need to make sure that you have a very solid foundation."

Why do I think my needs can best be addressed by a partnership or alliance?

Before advancing a partnership or alliance, entrepreneurs should ask whether that is the best structure for the relationship. Are you better to acquire or will a less formal collaboration work better? "We have had many failed partnerships; we also have many successful ones," says Olivia Lum of Hyflux. "I find that a partnership is sometimes about culture. I may be the best of partners at the CEO level but sometimes because the Singaporean culture is different from other cultures, such as the Western culture, it could be my people who sometimes create a lot of tension. I must also take some blame because maybe in hindsight we should not have partnered; we should just take on a loose collaboration rather than a partnership."

When do I want the relationship to begin and how long should it continue?

Just as in some cultures couples may live together before marrying, so too there is often value in having less formal working relationships between organizations and teams before entering into a more formal alliance or partnership. Try before you buy.

"We have had very long term relationships with our Danish partners (24 years)," says Rosario Bazán of DanPer. "This has been a very successful partnership because we started by getting to know each other as people before becoming partners. It was very important that we had the same values, especially around honesty, respect, and commitment. From then on, we developed a shared vision that we both identified. Our relationship is based on confidence, transparency, and open books. The global financial institutions that have funded us have been able to see how well the Danish and Peruvians have been able to work together."

Who will be responsible on both sides for managing the relationship?

Relationships function best when there are clear roles and responsibilities and when there is open, healthy communication between parties. Entrepreneurs attest to the importance of these characteristics in successful business partnerships and alliances. "Communication is vital to the success of alliances," says Dame Rosemary Squire of Trafalgar Entertainment Group, and she should know since theater productions involve countless collaborative relationships, each making a unique and vital contribution to the whole.

Transaction effectiveness

The Entrepreneurs don't just execute transactions; they focus on effectively integrating them into their existing business operations, creating comprehensive post-merger integration plans to capture synergies and eliminate redundancies. They develop key metrics to assess and monitor integration performance, and strong governance structures and processes to ensure that goals and milestones are achieved.

Maximizing transaction value

Once a potential transaction has been identified and the strategic fit has been evaluated and validated, the Entrepreneurs focus on how the transaction should be structured and valued to maximize returns. Entrepreneurs understand that a good deal is always good for all parties, not just themselves. A relationship that starts from a position of fairness has a much better chance of success than one that has inequality built in from the start.

"I don't know the number, but I think we have acquired over 100 company assets over 32 years," says Mohed Altrad. "It's been a big part of our life. You first need a solid base and respect for whom you are going to acquire. You need to look for solid growth, internal growth, and good profitability. Are the people happy and willing to work for you? Are the clients and suppliers happy? Is the company living in peace, not cheating anyone, and paying its taxes? Are they offering their clients top-class service and how are they doing this? It's about a solid base because to be successful you need your employees to be happy too."

Structuring the transaction

The Entrepreneurs pay careful attention to structuring transactions and alliances, taking into account factors such as tax optimization, risk management, local laws, regulations and business practices, financing alternatives, and employee incentives. It's also important for the structure to be simple and transparent to all parties.

"Our business is really simple," says Timothy Sloan, CFO of Wells Fargo. "When you look at a deal and its structure looks like an octopus or spider, just don't do it."[1]

Valuing the target

There is a limit to what any potential acquisition is really worth. Some targets have a value to financial buyers that may be lower than the value to strategic buyers because of the synergies and cost savings that strategic buyers, like the Entrepreneurs, will be able to realize. Their advice is to be realistic and not to overestimate the value of those synergies, or the time and cost that will be required to truly realize them.

---

[1] Katya Wachtel, "Wells Fargo CFO Explains the One and Only Way to Avoid a Horrible Deal," *Business Insider*, March 10, 2011.

Due diligence, deal negotiation, and structuring

Once the potential acquirer has determined a fair range of value that they would be prepared to pay for the target, deal negotiation and structuring starts. At any point in this process, often as a result of due diligence, things may come to light – about people, customers, brand and reputation, adequacy of supply chain, ownership of intellectual property, and many other things – that are a cause for pause. Typically such items result in an adjustment of the price, a revision in the terms and conditions, or termination of negotiations. Successful entrepreneurs – in the words of the great Kenny Rogers song – "Know when to hold 'em and know when to fold 'em." Being clear about the things that would be deal breakers from the onset will help to make such decisions in the moment. The master deal maker Murad Al-Katib says, "[An] important lesson I learned was don't ever fall in love with your takeover targets. Always be willing to walk away."

Jim Nixon of Nixon Energy Investments puts it a different way: "Have a very healthy scepticism and be prepared that you will find some surprises in the first hundred days. Some good and some bad. Generally speaking, if you have done enough diligence then the good will balance the bad."

Integrating the business and extracting intended value

Well before you ink the deal, you'll have developed a plan to integrate the acquired business into your company to maximize value. While the plan generally spans months or years, the first 100 days are critical. Our exceptional Entrepreneurs develop a 100-day plan designed to preserve and extract the most value out of acquisitions. When it comes to dealmaking, the devil really is in the details.

"It's about targeting, it's about building relationships, it's about having conviction that this is the right thing for you, and then executing to the minute detail – and that's how acquisitions work. The reason most acquisitions fail is that people miss the execution of the detail," advises Uday Kotak of Kotak Mahindra Bank.

Sometimes, after a spate of energetic dealmaking, you need to hit the pause button. Integrating multiple businesses in rapid succession is both difficult and resource intensive.

As with partnerships and alliances, it is critical to set targets and establish metrics that evaluate the success of each transaction. These could include growth in revenue, accretive earnings, synergies, and cost savings, for example. It is important to have a structured review and feedback loop in place to determine whether estimates that were used in establishing valuation and time frames predicted have come to fruition. Gaps between expectations and performance can offer great learning opportunities to feed into a future acquisition strategy.

The Entrepreneurs we interviewed have used a wide range of transactions and alliances to transform, add credibility to, and accelerate the growth of their businesses. They have shown us how to source the right transactions, pay the right price, and execute the deal at the right time. They then properly integrate them into their existing businesses to create maximum value. The last words of the chapter, however, sound a note of caution. As President Donald Trump admonishes, "Sometimes your best investments are the ones you don't make."[2]

---

[2] https://www.forbes.com/quotes/2205.

13

Driver #7: Risk

"Threat or opportunity"

This is a difficult driver for the natural-born entrepreneur to grasp: surely entrepreneurship is all about risking it? As Richard Branson, founder of Virgin Group, is fond of saying "Screw it! Let's do it!" And yet growth stories, like all stories, tell how our heroes guard against all manner of risks and dark forces. Managing risk is as important as managing opportunity, if not as much fun.

"Entrepreneurs are risk takers," says Randy Tavierne, EY Global Leader, Growth Markets Assurance, "but the best high-growth entrepreneurs also understand the importance of risk management – and put in place people, process, and technology to manage risk effectively. The benefits are many, including more rapid access to capital and a lower cost associated with that capital."

As shown in Figure 13.1, regardless of a company's stage of growth, the ability to identify and manage risk is essential to

Leading
Functions work together to deliver efficient and effective enterprise-wide risk management. This results in a lower cost of capital and improved business performance.

Established
There are formal roles and functions to address risks. Typically, these operate independently.

Developing
Management fully understands key risks and shares responsibility for them.

FIGURE 13.1 EY 7 Drivers of Growth – Risk

sustainable success. Company leaders with the ambition to become market leaders should not fear risk, but they should recognize that it exists. Identifying risk, implementing sound policies to mitigate it, and being aware that any risk management strategy will need continual review frees up the business to focus on opportunity.

Entrepreneurial success in the area of risk is dependent on successful implementation in four key areas:

- Risk identification
- Policies, procedures, and compliance
- Stakeholder management
- Governance

Risk comes in many forms – strategic, credit, market, financial, operational, cyber, reputational, and compliance. Successful entrepreneurs actively assess, monitor, and mitigate potential risks through an enterprise risk management framework, and communicate ongoing risk management practices to key stakeholders and all their employees. Risk is particularly an area where the weakest link may not be an external offensive threat, but a lax internal one.

Creating value from risk management

The Entrepreneurs interviewed for this book adopt a different approach to risk than do many of their peers. They embrace risk, they hire people willing to take risks, and their very existence is defined by a willingness to take risks. They create a very positive risk culture within their business and, importantly, they really understand how to take calculated risks to achieve their financial and growth goals.

"Don't be afraid to take a chance," suggests Linda Hasenfratz of Linamar. "As an entrepreneur, you are inherently going to be a bit of a risk taker; you must take a risk. You don't have to bet the farm, but you need to take risk and don't be afraid to give it a try – because you miss 100% of the shots you don't take." Notice, however, that Linda Hasenfratz doesn't advocate blind risk taking. Not betting the farm – assessing the potential downside and whether the entrepreneur and the company can live with it – is a matter of judgment.

"You and I could talk about something today and your perception could be 'low risk' and mine could be that it's 'high risk,'" says Craig Heatley of Rainbow Corporation and SKY TV. "So it's all relative, right? Everyone's perception of the word 'risk' is different, and so it's dangerous to talk about risk as a generic. It is not. Now personalize it and ask yourself, 'What is my definition of risk?' I don't believe I am a risk taker, other people say I am, because their perception of some of the things I have done is that they were risky. My perception is that they were not risky. I am a pilot, I am trained not to take risk."

Like pilots, entrepreneurs, who risk a lot much of the time, have to be excellent risk managers. "I think you start off as a risk taker and you acquire a risk management capability over time during the journey," says Jim Nixon. "If you get to a place where you are maybe a 30% risk taker and 70% a risk manager, you have found the balance."

Our research shows that businesses that manage risk well outperform their competitors with better profits, more predictable growth, and more efficient use of capital. They reduce the volatility in the business. The Entrepreneurs we interviewed understand this. Investors and analysts look for good risk management and the cost of capital for companies that demonstrate this is lower. For those looking to exit, strong risk management is an essential indicator of a well-run business that has a very positive outcome on valuations.

While for many, risk management is a necessary burden, the Entrepreneurs we interviewed understand the importance of embedding good risk management and a culture of responsible risk taking throughout the business. They consider and manage risks in everything they do, across all core functions and processes.

"You need to do a good job of identifying risk and that's not something that can be done by a corporate department; you need everybody's involvement," points out Linda Hasenfratz. "To tease out risks, whether they be around markets, people, currencies, or customers, we need to get input from the ground and then we can see where there are issues developing. The risk may be across just one facility or many smaller issues which pooled together turns into something that might be a more serious risk. It's important to develop strategies to mitigate those risks."

Stakeholder management

As we have seen, as a business grows so does the pool of stakeholders the business has to manage. In the early days, the primary stakeholders are those who have provided initial capital (friends, family, angel investors, banks, etc.), employees, customers, and suppliers. The most important stories that need to be told are about the product or service. Does it work? Does it sell? Is the pricing right? Who is buying it? Stakeholders will be keen to know that all of the key business risks are understood and managed by leaders.

As the business develops, the stakeholders group will broaden. New funding sources will have a more detailed interest in the business. They will want to understand the strategy and goals for growth. They will want to know that leaders are able to deliver against their promises for both revenue and profit. They will be keen to hear about new strategic hires, possible acquisition targets, and strategies to manage risk. There will be expectation that management will be proactive in reporting and explaining major developments, both negative and positive.

"As a measure of how far I have come, 30 years ago I could not find a bank to lend me €7,000; today two banks and the French government are my business partners," says Mohed Altrad, illustrating how his business has shifted over time.

Finally, as a company achieves scale, it needs to engage with the communities that it is part of and serves. It will communicate its corporate social responsibility measures and engage with regulators and policy makers and will seek to influence policy.

At each stage, communicating how the company is managing risk is important.

Policies, procedures, and compliance

Most early-stage businesses do one thing very well – they ensure that key risks for the business are fully understood and managed by someone in the leadership team. As they grow, they create roles to manage them and, ultimately, connect various risk and compliance functions under a common risk framework so that a proper perspective on policies, procedures, and compliance is embedded in the culture. Risks are well understood and people know how to appropriately respond in the event of an unanticipated situation.

"One of the main ways we have reduced our risk in our 48 operations is by never compromising safety," says Murad Al-Katib of AGT. "We demand safety programs in every country that we operate. There are two elements, emotional.... I don't ever want to be the one who has to make a call to a family and tell them how their loved one was harmed at work, but on the other side, there is enterprise risk too. It's reputation, it's regulatory, and it's the right thing to identify those risks, manage them, and be very predictive in that ability – and to ensure we identify the risks, but at the same time understanding them and having policies that we manage and test. I think this has been a very important and strong strategy."

Exceptional entrepreneurs have a structured approach to regularly identifying, monitoring, and assessing key risks. They embed risk management into the operational culture of the business and they ensure that leadership sets the tone at the top. They also tell the story of how they manage risk to key stakeholders – especially investor communities. Our research shows that those who do achieve this have a lower cost of capital.

Many businesses suffer the burden of complex regulations that prevail within many industry sectors. The Entrepreneurs try to look beyond compliance and work with regulators and peers to shape the nature of future policy.

Governance

Effective risk management requires a strong internal oversight structure, one that promotes risk accountability, a strong risk culture, and adherence to the firm's risk appetite framework.

Successful entrepreneurs put in place governing bodies (such as boards of directors, usually including experienced, well-qualified, independent, external board members) and/or a risk management function. A clearly defined operating model helps ensure the organization is able to make decisions that balance risk considerations with competitive realities to drive better business outcomes.

Entrepreneurs are risk takers. But those who enjoy sustainable success take risks in order to seize opportunities; they understand that risks are endemic and put in place a comprehensive approach to managing them. As Warren Buffett, investor and CEO of Berkshire Hathaway, says, "Risk comes from not knowing what you're doing."

*   *   *

EY 7 Drivers of Growth: many success stories

In this and the preceding chapters, we have shared our insights and the real-life experiences of the exceptional Entrepreneurs in building their extraordinary companies. Our experience of working with many hundreds of clients across the world has resulted in the EY 7 Drivers of Growth framework. Each driver interconnects with the others. Companies looking to develop partnerships and alliances will need to build funding and finance; having good risk management processes will need to be embedded in operations; good digital capability will underpin every aspect of the business; every driver needs the best talent to implement the corporate vision; putting customers at the center is nonoptional. Just as gears work together to drive a machine, so the 7 drivers work together to drive growth.

Traits, skills, and the importance of intuition

In the earlier chapters of this book, we identified traits that our award-winning Entrepreneurs share, as well as the operational capabilities they have deployed encapsulated in the EY 7 Drivers of Growth framework. What was it that spurred them to dare to compete and then what specific skills did they need to execute on their grand vision? In our final chapter we integrate all these different elements in what we hope will be a useful synthesis of theory and experience – a deep understanding of what it takes to build an exceptional business from the kitchen table to market leadership.

World-class Entrepreneurs and building sustainable market-leading companies

F or all of us, behaviors are shaped by the personal traits we are born with, then are developed through our life experiences and the knowledge and skills we accumulate from formal and informal learning. World-class Entrepreneurs are influenced by all these factors, but through writing this book we have learned that they also rely on another, very powerful force.

As you seek to accelerate the growth of your business, ask yourself how you can further develop the traits of a great entrepreneur, expand your knowledge and application of the EY 7 Drivers of Growth, and learn to rely more heavily on another vital enabler.

In Part 1, we outlined the criteria that our EY World Entrepreneur Of The Year independent judging panel uses to select the annual winner: entrepreneurial spirit, value creation, strategic direction, national and global impact, innovation, and personal integrity / purpose-driven leadership. How are you developing each of these in your own personal and entrepreneurial life?

We discussed the DNA of a successful high-growth entrepreneur – traits that reflect the essence of a truly great entrepreneur. These were distilled from our interviews with the Entrepreneurs and included inspirational leadership, passion and drive, vision and focus, hunger for learning, resilience, purpose, and agility.

Through the discussion of the stories of the Entrepreneurs, we have illustrated how each of them, on a daily basis, is daring to compete and how the traits described above are elemental to who they are and how they operate.

In the 7 Drivers of Growth chapters we explained the knowledge and skills that successful entrepreneurs use to accelerate growth and showed how the Entrepreneurs apply these drivers in making business decisions. Are you applying the 7 Drivers of Growth to your company?

In this chapter we ask, what else truly differentiates those that become world-class, high-growth entrepreneurs? And how can you learn from and apply this knowledge to enhance your own entrepreneurial journey?

No excuses!

The Entrepreneurs we interviewed have a broad range of early childhood and family experiences. They achieved a variety of levels of educational attainment. Their lives and businesses grew in geographies that spanned the globe. And yet all have become extraordinarily successful. What distinguishes great entrepreneurs is not where they come from, but where they are going. Thankfully, the same is true for all of us. We can't choose where we come from but we can choose what to do with our lives.

Some aspects of the E-gene presented early in life – well before these superstars ever began building their ultimate businesses. Their early life interests, activities, and experiences, coupled with family and personal values, shaped the Entrepreneurs and the businesses they ultimately built.

Is it nature or nurture? Who knows? What we can say is that an affinity for being an entrepreneur shows up early in life.

Four-year-old Declan is the oldest grandson of Bryan Pearce, EY Global Leader, Entrepreneurship, and coauthor of this book. Of his own volition – with no prompting from parents or grandparents – Declan wanted set up an "energy-bite" stand on his driveway to earn money "to buy Legos" (see Figure 14.1). When one husband and wife pulled up in their car and the husband got out to buy one bag, Declan – showing his sales

FIGURE 14.1 Declan

skills – asked him if he also wanted to "buy a bag for her." His entrepreneurial instincts have emerged early and who knows how he will apply these later in life.

We can all encourage young entrepreneurs: parents, teachers, policy makers, and serial entrepreneurs can help keep the flame alive.

Necessity and survival are strong motivators

Mohed Altrad and Olivia Lum had the worst possible starts in life. Neither of them knew their biological parents and both were brought up by elderly women with no knowledge of the world beyond the shacks they called home. As young children, both were consumed by the need to survive.

"In my early life, I was struggling just to eat and drink," Mohed Altrad says. Olivia Lum recalls, "We were so poor we lived in a tiny house with no electricity or running water. We had to find our food from local charities." Both had a daily fight for survival. There was little encouragement to learn and yet both found ways, against all the odds, to outperform their peers and excel academically. Each abandoned stable and promising careers with employers to build their own hugely successful businesses and both have been EY World Entrepreneur Of The Year winners.

What their stories tell us is that you don't choose your start in life, but you do choose what to make of your life.

A strong work ethic and a deep sense of personal responsibility

Manny Stul started life in a refugee camp in Germany. After moving to Australia, he and his family found themselves living in disused army barracks. But each of his parents had an extraordinary work ethic. His father was a cabinetmaker and his mother a packer in a chemical factory; they were self-taught, but had great respect for education and had accumulated extraordinary general knowledge.

Jim Nixon, Craig Heatley, and Lonnie Moulder all started their business lives selling newspapers. Jim Nixon and Craig Heatley lost their fathers when they were young, but not before the sons had seen firsthand what it meant to support families with long hours and hard work. Nixon's father was a butcher supporting eight children, and Heatley's was in the Army. Lonnie Moulder's father didn't finish high school and supplemented the family's income by working a second job as a cleaner in the evenings. All three were deeply loved by their mothers and felt a strong sense of responsibility for their siblings. Their work ethic was ingrained almost from birth.

Personal attitudes to work and a strong sense of values are embedded in us early on. You can learn almost anything with a will, but a strong work ethic and sense of responsibility – attributes that every successful entrepreneur shows – are foundational.

Competitive spirit

As a young person Manny Stul was very competitive, playing sports and chess with equal vigor, and joining in with any game he could find. He disliked high school but loved social activities. It's not surprising that his love of sports and games, coupled with his competitive need to win and his family values of honesty, tenacity, innovation, and creativity, have seen him build one of the world's largest toy companies.

Great entrepreneurs love to win.

Natural curiosity and a desire to understand how things work and fix them if they don't

Both Jim Nixon and Lonnie Moulder were taking engines apart and putting them back together from an early age. Moulder says, "I was always fascinated with how things worked and would disassemble various mechanical or electronic items, hoping to restore them to full functionality. When I was 11, I wanted a mini motorcycle, not just because it would be fun to ride on, but I couldn't wait to break down the engine in order to fully understand how it worked." Today, that's what he is doing with the human body.

Jim Nixon remembers, "I had my first motorcycle at 13 and my mother used to let me bring it into the back hallway, take it apart, and put it back together." Such early tinkering led Nixon to build some of the world's best known mechanical engineering companies.

As a small child Rubens Menin's mother taught him calculus and he visited engineering projects with his father and grandfather. He could see the physical manifestations of the theoretical math his mother was teaching him. It's no surprise then that he became the most famous engineer in Latin America and the EY World Entrepreneur Of The Year 2018 – a title he earned not just for his successful business but for his dedication to ensuring that home ownership would become a reality for the poorest people in Brazil. He accepted the honor with his trademark humility.

When Uday Kotak was 10 years old he started to read financial newspapers and devoured every piece of information he could find on Wall Street. Today he controls the fourth largest private bank in India with assets of more than US$20 billion.

Michael Wu remembers following his grandfather into the family's restaurants to taste the food and talk to the chefs. He was taught to be critical of every single dish. Today he has grown that enterprise into a multinational group with 32,000 employees, characterized by innovation and creativity.

Looking back, it seems that Linda Hasenfratz was destined to head up her father's auto engineering business. While other young women were studying "softer" subjects, Linda was pursuing studies in physics, chemistry, and math. She took calculus at the university level, just because she enjoyed it. Those tough math-based subjects, together with her personal values of honor, decency, and empathy, took her to the C-suite, leading a company with multibillion dollar sales.

Great entrepreneurs are builders – instinctively accumulating experiences that become the blocks with which they build exceptional businesses.

A desire to solve problems, correct unfairness, and improve communities by fighting for what you believe in

The abject poverty Mohed Altrad and Olivia Lum experienced in their early lives gave them a lens through which to view the world. Trying to reduce injustice in society drove them to create businesses where the principles of fairness, forgiveness, and fortitude are paramount in everything they do.

Rosario Bazán's business values, performance, and behavior derive directly from the values she learned at home during childhood. As the eighth of 11 children, she learned how to conciliate, "looking for peace." She learned how to compete and fight in a fair way, developing a strong values framework that shaped her character and her business. When she had to fight her way back from the loss of her first enterprise, she had the inner strength to do so.

As a teenager, Murad Al-Katib realized he was a better sports coach than player, and spent his teenage years "working to make his community a better place." By his early 40s, he had been awarded the Oslo Business for Peace Award for his extraordinary charity in helping eradicate poverty. In the same year (2017) he became EY World Entrepreneur Of The Year.

Mary Lynne Hedley says, "My values in part were acquired by experiences I had growing up, and ensured that my life path would involve doing something to improve that path for others. I can still see myself at age 10, with my sisters and brothers all piled into our station wagon with a pile of Christmas presents, singing carols and traveling on a snowy Christmas Eve down an unpaved road, into a community of small, ramshackle buildings. Confused, but confident in my parents, we all tumbled out and gathered presents from the car trunk. I will not forget the darkness, the one bed, the scant furniture, the lack of 'stuff.' We arranged the packages on the single table; there was no Christmas tree." Today Hedley is still delivering life-changing packages. They are called anticancer drugs.

Entrepreneurs often start a business because of their desire to satisfy an unmet need in the market.

Self-confidence

As Uday Kotak says, "chasing something beyond money" and leading from the front with innate self-confidence is a driving force.

By the time she was 16, Dame Rosemary Squire was sitting on the Playhouse Theatre steps with enough self-assurance to know that the theater was where she wanted to make her life. She went on to study modern languages and is now described by many, including London's *Evening Standard*, as "the most influential woman in theater of all time."

Great entrepreneurs believe in themselves and their ability to realize their vision.

Understand the power of the kitchen table effect

Those Entrepreneurs who were fortunate to have families that provided a supportive upbringing learned values and attitudes by being around the kitchen table at home. Dame Rosemary Squire, Rosario Bazán, Murad Al-Katib, Rubens Menin, Uday Kotak, Michael Wu, Linda Hasenfratz, Ilkka Paananen, and Mary Lynne Hedley were fortunate to come from families where higher education was valued and a given and where parental support was unwavering. They were loved, nurtured, encouraged, and exposed to great role models who gave them strong foundations on which to build their lives.

Entrepreneurs know that great businesses, like happy families, are underpinned by principles of reliability, honesty, and compassion. They show respect for people and for them, it's not what they have, but who they are that matters.

Integrity

In our interviews, the Entrepreneurs used the word "integrity" again and again. The word literally means being whole and undivided. There are those who believe "entrepreneur" stands for grasping acquisitiveness, a person focused on self-gain with no scruples. Indeed, Olivia Lum was told by one of her university professors that it was unthinkable to be an entrepreneur for precisely this reason.

But the winning Entrepreneurs profiled in this book, including Lum, prove that personal integrity is a vital part of the entrepreneurial spirit. These people have achieved all they have achieved because integrity is hardwired into their DNA, and none of them have pursued growth from a motive to get rich.

To be the best in the world, not only have the Entrepreneurs surrounded themselves with the best teams but, when choosing those team members, they have selected people with integrity too. There is an old Spanish proverb, "Tell me who you walk with and I will tell you who you are." Truly successful entrepreneurs only want to walk with stakeholders who share their commitment to integrity.

The size and scale of the businesses the Entrepreneurs have created is not an accident. None has gotten rich quick, but all have amassed wealth by never compromising their personal integrity or that of their company.

Leadership

Ilkka Paananen's military training stood him in good stead for his entrepreneurial career. He says, "When you are leading people who are not getting paid and you want them to follow you into battle, you learn a lot about motivation." His aspirations and personal courage have seen him start a business (Supercell) that is described by some as "The most profitable business (per employee) in the world."

Entrepreneurs bring all of their traits and knowledge together to build and lead outstanding teams who share their vision and passion.

No matter where your entrepreneurial journey begins, or where you are along its path, focus on developing and strengthening these traits and applying the 7 Drivers of Growth to accelerate the growth of your business.

Intuition

As we stated at the conclusion of Chapter 3, in all of our discussions of motivation, character traits, early upbringing, and business capabilities, there is one unique ingredient of the DNA of Entrepreneurs that we have not yet explored: intuition. Intuition, instinct, sixth sense – call it what you will – has played a massive role in helping our Entrepreneurs make the right decisions at the right time with the right partner. While some may play down the importance of something as nebulous and difficult to quantify as intuition, through our interviews with these exceptional Entrepreneurs we have seen that learning to trust your gut is as important to their success as all the other factors identified in these chapters.

Craig Heatley, founder, Rainbow Corporation and SKY TV: "What is intuition? It could be a combination of other senses. We know our five senses – those are obvious. But we have other senses which some of us are more in tune with than others. Head versus heart is no contest. Not everything is explicable. I accept that there is stuff we can't explain. Instinct, intuition – when I hear that inner voice, I have learned to follow it. Maybe we are not as in control as we think we are. There are a lot of things we don't know. Listen to your heart. I have made my biggest mistakes by listening to my head. Listen to your heart first even if you don't know where it's taking you."

Dame Rosemary Squire, Trafalgar Entertainment Group:
"You need intuition to recognize a good opportunity and then you need the imagination to add color, to look at it, examine it, develop it, and make it complete. Also important are hard work, being prepared, resilience, and knowing where you are headed. If you have done your due diligence, if you are on top of your numbers, you know your subject matter, and if your intuition says this is going to help me get to my destination, then you are in a very strong position to succeed."

Ilkka Paananen, Supercell: "Intuition has played a big role in my success. It develops with experience, as you encounter similar situations that you have been in before. It took me a while to start trusting my intuition. Some advice I would give to others is not to blindly listen to advice from successful people but learn to trust your own intuition."

Jim Nixon, Nixon Energy Investments: "Intuition is something I feel strongly about. Intuition is a feeling through the subconscious mind that can help you create a reality. If you are in doubt, always go with your intuition. If you can't explain why you want to do something, there is usually a good intuitive reason behind that and it's usually the right thing to do. I think you have to be careful that as you progress as an entrepreneur, you don't let that intuition dissipate and work purely on facts, numbers, and data – because it's the intuition that got you there in the first place."

Linda Hasenfratz, Linamar Corporation: "I think intuition, or maybe call it instinct, is something that develops over time with experience. I think it's something you get better and better at. The older you get, the more experience you have, the more ups and downs that you have been through, the more good and bad hires you have made – this all helps you to develop those instincts and intuitions. I think it's important that you look for the little red flags or listen to the little voice in your head because sometimes when I have failed to do so I have paid the price."

Manny Stul, Moose Toys: "Intuition is probably a feeling, an emotion, a comfort. You know when something is right. I think it's a combination of your past experiences; it's almost getting into contact with your spiritual side. It's an energy thing. You feel it when you meet someone, and it doesn't feel quite right; it's like their energy doesn't synch with yours." He says, "Not many people are aware of their intuition. They tend to be guided by logic, facts and figures, and what other people think. But if you are a true entrepreneur then your main guide will be your intuition."

Michael Wu, Maxim Group: "I get my inspiration through traveling around the world, gaining exposure to new trends and changes in consumer behavior. Experience, experimentation, and learning from mistakes help sharpen my intuition. The most important thing, though, is not the idea, but how you put that into practice."

Mohed Altrad, The Altrad Group: "If you look at my original Arabic culture, it's not rational. Only 20% of what I do is rational. When I bought my first business it was in a mess. I came from a computer science background and knew nothing about scaffolding. So, on the face of it, the purchase was not rational. But I could 'see' the various elements needed for the business to succeed, so my first reaction was to believe in myself and believe in my dreams."

Murad Al-Katib, AGT Food and Ingredients, Inc: "Do your homework, have no fear, and know the outcomes you want. But if my heart – my gut feeling – does not feel right with it, then I walk away because I think your heart and gut feel things your brain is unable to properly synthesize. So, intuition is vital to take into account."

Olivia Lum, Hyflux Ltd.: "I feel that many times you don't know what works, and sometimes things don't turn out, but intuition will allow you to at least have a go at something. If you don't have intuition you have to depend on report after report to give you analysis of whether something will work or not. Intuition is somehow already part of your DNA. So your eyes are already wide open. If you are an entrepreneur and you firmly believe something will work, you will go all out."

Rosario Bazán, DanPer: "We hear all the time that women develop intuition to a higher level than men. I really don't know about that but what I do know is that my intuition has played a very important role in running my business – especially when this intuition is clearly linked to experience, to knowledge, and interaction with people that are in the business. It's hard to explain but I just have a feeling and listen to it."

Mary Lynne Hedley, TESARO, Inc.: "I think intuition has played a large part in my success. I think that it helps in creating a vision, taking things that are perhaps unrelated, and seeing how these things might come together. I also think it's a skill in the sense that the more I have trusted my intuition, the bigger the next leap I am willing to take. It's an exercise like a muscle."

Lonnie Moulder, TESARO, Inc.: "I think intuition is very important and, if you think it through, intuition is really subconsciously bringing together all your knowledge and experience in a quick decision. It's something that is developed over time. It means you are not consciously having to go through the whole rational process of thinking about something because it just happens."

Uday Kotak, Kotak Mahindra Bank: "Call it intuition, call it opportunity, it never announces when it comes. I think intuition is very important, but it also has to have a fair dose of risk management, because it depends on how you look at intuition and how you manage it. Getting the mix right is extremely important for getting a high probability of success. I think taking a bet on your convictions is a good thing but the line between convictions and foolhardiness is very thin."

Rubens Menin, MRV Engenharia: "I truly believe in intuition … there are occasions or situations when there were doubts about which options to choose, and intuition helped me to make the right choice."

In summary, the Entrepreneurs agree – to sustain success in life and in business you need intuition and the courage to listen to that inner voice. Belief in the importance of intuition can also be found in great leaders in fields such as politics, the military, medicine, and sport.

Jim Nixon argues that it is this trust in intuition that characterizes the true entrepreneur. "I think there is a difference between a business person and an entrepreneur," he says. "You can be a great business person but not an entrepreneur. As a business person, your primary movers are management systems, processes, and people. But entrepreneurs are intuitive and break the mold – they change something and make it different."

To better accelerate the growth of your business and continue daring to compete, develop your entrepreneurial traits, execute against the EY 7 Drivers of Growth, and attune your decision making to that inner voice of intuition. When all is said and done, the Entrepreneurs listen to their hearts over their heads. No matter how extensive the analysis … it is you out there. On your own. You have to own your own decisions. Trust yourself and let your intuition be your final guide.

*   *   *

The beginning . . .

Appendix

Information on applying to the EY Entrepreneur Of The Year program or accessing our EY 7 Drivers of Growth™

We hope that as a result of reading this book and being inspired by the stories of the 15 EY Entrepreneur Of The Year winners that we interviewed – that you will consider nominating yourself or a great entrepreneur that you know for the program. For information on the EY Entrepreneur Of The Year program please visit https://www.ey.com/entrepreneurship.

Many of you will want to assess your business against the EY 7 Drivers of Growth™. This can be done through an in-person meeting that can be arranged by contacting your nearest EY office (see www.ey.com), or by joining EY Velocity at www.ey.com/Velocity and signing up. Here you will be able to access and continually update your activities and progress relating to the EY 7 Drivers of Growth™ and access other valuable resources.

About the authors

Diane Foreman

Diane Foreman is one of New Zealand's leading business people. Since her time as Vice Chairman of the NZ Business Roundtable in the heady days of the 1990s, she and her businesses have been named NZ Exporter of the Year and NZ Franchisor of the Year. Diane was created a Companion of the New Zealand Order of Merit for her Services to Business and named by *Forbes* Magazine as one of the 40 most influential women in Asia.

Over 30 years Diane has amassed a vast range of business credentials including healthcare, manufacturing, franchising, recruitment, hotels, and property development. Through her family owned companies she has owned and operated businesses in NZ, Australia, China, the United States, England, and Europe.

Since winning EY Entrepreneur of the Year™ 2009 New Zealand, Diane has been a judge for the EY World Entrepreneur Of The Year competition.

Bryan Pearce

EY Global Leader – Entrepreneurship and Start-Ups

Bryan leads EY Entrepreneur Of The Year™, the world's most prestigious business awards program for entrepreneurs. For more than 30 years, EY Entrepreneur Of The Year has celebrated those who are building and leading successful, high-growth businesses, recognizing them through awards programs in more than 50 countries and 145 cities, culminating each June with the EY World Entrepreneur Of The Year™ in Monaco. In this role, Bryan has built a network of relationships with outstanding entrepreneurs around the world and a deep understanding of the challenges and opportunities they face.

Bryan also leads EY's global initiatives to help start-up companies accelerate their growth, and co-founded EY Velocity: a comprehensive web portal that provides resources to accelerate the growth of entrepreneurial companies.

Bryan shares his knowledge of entrepreneurship, start-ups, and venture financing as a commentator in the media, and lectures on these topics at universities and conferences.

A passionate believer in the power of entrepreneurship at all levels, Bryan has served as Chair of the Network for Teaching Entrepreneurship in New England, is an active member of Vistage International, and manages EY's relationship with Endeavor.

Bryan graduated from the Richard Ivey School of Business at the University of Western Ontario, and he currently sits on the Ivey Business School Advisory Board, and is a Canadian Chartered Professional Accountant.

Geoffrey Godding

EY Global Digital & Innovation Leader – Growth Markets

As author of the EY 7 Drivers of Growth™, Geoffrey led the development of global deployment of EY 7 Drivers of Growth digital assessment, a technology-enabled approach which uses the drivers to transform the way that business leaders think about and achieve growth on their journey from start-up to market leadership. He is also the co-founder of EY Velocity, a unique digital portal for entrepreneurs. Through both of these initiatives he brings innovative ways for EY to support leaders of high-growth businesses.

An EY partner for more than 20 years, Geoffrey has had a long and varied career in management consultancy, working with a wide range of clients from start-ups to market leaders across the world.

Prior to EY, Geoffrey held leadership positions in two start-up and high-growth consultancy businesses, which gave him hands-on experience of the challenges facing entrepreneurs.

He holds a Leading Professional Services Diploma from Harvard Business School and a degree in Pure Mathematics and Statistics from the University of Exeter.

About EY

EY is a global leader in assurance, tax, transaction, and advisory services. The insights and quality services we deliver help build trust and confidence in the capital markets and in economies the world over. We develop outstanding leaders who team to deliver on our promises to all of our stakeholders. In so doing, we play a critical role in building a better working world for our people, for our clients, and for our communities.

EY refers to the global organization, and may refer to one or more of the member firms of Ernst & Young Global Limited, each of which is a separate legal entity. Ernst & Young Global Limited, a UK company limited by guarantee, does not provide services to clients. For more information about our organization, please visit ey.com.

Index